A CHANCE TO SET
THE RECORD STRAIGHT

Jack Nicklaus, Larry Bird, Martina Navratilova, Walter Payton, Pete Rose, Wayne Gretzky, Muhammad Ali, Eric Heiden, Roger Clemens, Jim Brown, Carl Lewis, Dwight Gooden, Kareem Abdul-Jabbar, Eric Dickerson, Babe Ruth, Bill Hartack, Michael Jordan, Gordie Howe, Joe Montana, Wilt Chamberlain, Boris Becker, A.J. Foyt, Jerry West . . .

Winners all, what they and the hundreds of other superstars here in THE ILLUSTRATED SPORTS RECORD BOOK have in common is a record (or several). Covering a broad range of sports, their history-making marks have set a standard for athletes to shoot at—and for you to use as a guide when watching your favorite sport.

THE
ILLUSTRATED SPORTS
RECORD BOOK

Updated and Revised

SPECTATORS SPORTS

☐ **THE COMPLETE HANDBOOK OF BASEBALL: 1987 EDITION edited by Zander Hollander.** The essential book for every baseball fan. Twenty-six team yearbooks in one, with nearly 300 player and manager profiles, year-by-year stats, all-time records and award winners, and hundreds of photos. (147618—$4.95)

☐ **SPORTS NOSTALGIA QUIZ BOOK (Revised and Updated Edition) by Zander Hollander and David Schulz.** Packed with entertainment and exciting memories. Great sports figures are recalled and thrilling athletic events recaptured as you dig deep into the old mental bean bag for answers to over 150 tantalizing quizzes. (140230—$2.50)

☐ **INSTANT REPLAY: THE GREEN BAY DIARY OF JERRY KRAMER edited by Dick Schaap.** From the locker room to the goal line, from the training field to the Super Bowl, this is the inside story of a great pro football team... "The best behind-the-scenes glimpse of pro football ever produced."—*The New York Times* (146301—$3.95)*

☐ **EVERYTHING YOU ALWAYS WANTED TO KNOW ABOUT SPORTS* *and didn't know where to ask by Mickey Herskowitz and Steve Perkins.** Here is the book that answers every question a sports fan ever had in the back of his mind and tells the truth about the whispered rumors of the sports world. (124715—$2.75)

THE ILLUSTRATED SPORTS RECORD BOOK

by Zander Hollander
and David Schulz

Updated and Revised Edition

AN ASSOCIATED FEATURES BOOK

A SIGNET BOOK

NEW AMERICAN LIBRARY

Copyright © 1975, 1987 by Associated Features, Inc.

 SIGNET TRADEMARK REG. U.S. PAT. OFF. AND FOREIGN COUNTRIES
REGISTERED TRADEMARK—MARCA REGISTRADA
HECHO EN CHICAGO, U.S.A.

SIGNET, SIGNET CLASSIC, MENTOR, ONYX, PLUME, MERIDIAN
and NAL BOOKS are published by NAL PENGUIN INC.,
1633 Broadway, New York, New York 10019

First Printing, September, 1975
First Printing (Updated and Revised Edition), June, 1987

2 3 4 5 6 7 8 9

PRINTED IN THE UNITED STATES OF AMERICA

CONTENTS

INTRODUCTION   xiii

BASEBALL

Iron Horse   3
Duffy's Day   3
The Kid Shoots for Seven   4
Rubber Arm   5
Cy Young's Last Game   5
Instant Major Leaguers   7
Rube the Great   8
Triple Threat   9
Goose Eggs in the Clutch   11
Streaking Giants   12
Three-Bag Man   13
Mr. 000 000 000   14
Babe on the Mound   14
On and On and On and On and   16
Sizzling Sisler   19
Boom-Boom Bottomley   19
End of the Line   20
Cobb's Corner   22
Ruthian Feat   23
Hack Performance   24
Fence Busters   24
The Bambino Bows Out   26
Lefty Is Right   28
Tiger, Tiger, Hitting Right   29
Dutch Treat   30
Foxx Trot   32
All-Star Hitter   34
Thank You, Mr. Pipp   34
Streaking Clipper   36
Indian Courage   37
Special Delivery   38

Splendid Splinter   39
12/13ths Perfect   41
Men for All Ages   42
Driving Them In   43
One Up on the Babe   44
Yogi's String   45
Changing of the Guard   47
Hitting the Wind   49
MOE-ing Them Down   51
A Long Time Coming   52
Dandy Don   54
All Over the Field   55
Gibby's ERA   55
Striking a Losing Pose   56
Night All-Stars   58
Say Hey, One More Time   59
Record Relief   61
Hank Hammers No. 755   61
Angel K   63
Mr. October   64
King of Thieves   65
Gooden Plenty   66
20 Whiffs   68
Horner's Homers   69
Fernando's Screwball   71
Charlie Hustle   72

PRO FOOTBALL

Nevers-Nevers Land   77
Hutson's Haul   77
Ram Catcher   79
Groundless Fears   80
The Flingin' Dutchman   81
On the Right Track   81
Golden Boy   83
Running Wild   84
Doing It Up Brown   85
Just for Kicks   85
Kapp-ital Performance   87
Mighty Foot   87
Starr Billing   90
Jack Be Nimble, Jack Be Quick   91
Return of the Cowboy   91

The Scrambler's Legacy   92
Ageless Viking   93
A Touch of Green   94
Have Gun, Will Shoot!   95
Return of the Century   95
Five for the Road   95
Bull's-Eye   97
Dorsett's Dash   97
Ali and "The Diesel"   100
Unbelievable Eric   101
Magnetic Monk   102
Splash of the Dolphins   102
Quick Ending   104
A Paige in the Book   105
Norwegian Boots   105
The Montana Miracle   105
Payton's Place   107
Soaring Seahawk   108
The Joiner Collection   108

PRO BASKETBALL

Carom King   111
All-Star Boardman   111
A 100 High   111
Making a Point   113
Sweet Charity   114
Deadly   114
End of Laker Chain   116
The Last Dip   116
Oscar Performance   119
West Is Best   121
Buckets by the Bushel   122
Longest Shot   124
A Porter's Job   124
Pure Calvin   124
A Smithian Streak   126
Best Bet   126
"The Big E"   127
Magic's Magic   128
Bird's Series Swoop   130
"The Mad Bomber"   131
Led by Isiah   132
Great Scott!   133

Kareem's Lot   133
Here Comes Mr. Jordan   135

HOCKEY

Goal-Getter   139
Canadien Goose Eggs   140
Puck Stopper   140
Tony Awards   141
Flyers' Hammer   143
Sittler's Explosion   143
Marathon Man   143
In the Penalty Box   145
Here's Howe   145
The Mark of a Tiger   147
The Great Gretzky   147

BOXING

Moore Knockouts   151
The Brockton Blockbuster   152
Ali's Triple   153

COLLEGE FOOTBALL

Mr. Inside and Mr. Outside   157
Mississippi Showboat   158
Jim Brown's Greatest Act   158
Rhome Not Built in a Day   160
Beware the Hurricane   161
Virgil's Standard   161
Pruitt Can Do It   163
Husker Hustler   163
Panther on the Prowl   164
Ivery Coasts   166
Sooner Boomer   166
McMahon Aloft   167
Young and Accurate   168
Rozier's Harvest   169
A-mayesing   169
Flutie Flips   171
Big Man on Little Campus   171

COLLEGE BASKETBALL

Backboard Dukes   177
Paladin's Gun   178
Tar Heel String   178
Carr's Finer Points   180
The Pistol's Parting Shots   181
Bruin Power   181
Runnin' (and Shootin') Rebels   184
Herculean Heave   185

TRACK AND FIELD

To the End of the Pit   189
Victory as Protest   189
Four for the Record   189
California Gold Rush   192

GOLF

"The Haig"   197
Link to Greatness   198
Queen of Swing   200
Wright On   201
Double Eagle from Taiwan   201
The Golden Bear   202

TENNIS

Moody Triumph   207
Rod's Slam   208
Court's Court   209
Boom Boom at Wimbledon   210
Martina's Destiny   211

HORSE RACING

Half-Dozen Roses   215
Majestic Hartack   216
Derby Double   217
Record Ride   218

AUTO RACING

Foyt's Fourth 500   223
Fastest Indy   224

SWIMMING

Spitz's Spritz   227

CYCLING

An American First in Paris   231

SPEED SKATING

Heiden's Sweep on Ice   235

THE ILLUSTRATED SPORTS RECORD BOOK

INTRODUCTION

Records, they say, are made to be broken. Hoss Radbourn would object to this thesis. Hoss, a pitcher for the National League's Providence team, won 60 games in a single season. That was in 1884, and the record stands.

So do such other vintage marks as Wilt Chamberlain's 100 points (and Frank Selvy's 100) in a basketball game; Gale Sayers's six touchdowns in a pro football game; Joe DiMaggio's 56-game hitting streak in baseball; UCLA's 88-game winning streak in basketball; Bobby Jones's golfing grand slam; Rod Laver's pair of tennis grand slams; and Bill Hartack's five victories in the Kentucky Derby.

These records have stood the test of time and assault by the new breed, but what is significant is that the modern superstars are dramatically whittling away at the old standards. This is evidenced by the fact that this second edition of *The Illustrated Sports Record Book* comprises more than 70 new stories with records that have been set since the book was first published in 1975.

They are among the nearly 200 stories and more than 350 records in this collection, which relates the various feats as they might have appeared at the time of achievement.

Our illustrious army of record-smashers continues to blend the stars of yesteryear with those of today—Babe Ruth, Sandy Koufax, and Hank Aaron with Pete Rose, Dwight Gooden, and Roger Clemens; Jimmy Brown, Paul Hornung, and Fran Tarkenton with Walter Payton, Joe Montana, and Eric Dickerson; Bob Pettit, Jerry West, and Oscar Robertson with Larry Bird, Michael Jordan, and Kareem Abdul-Jabbar; Gordie Howe and Terry Sawchuk with Wayne Gretzky; Rocky Marciano with Muhammad Ali; Bob Beamon with Carl Lewis; Walter Hagen and Mickey Wright with Jack Nicklaus; Helen Wills Moody with Martina Navratilova and Boris Becker; Eddie Arcaro with Chris McCarron; and such others as Mark Spitz and Eric Heiden.

They represent only a partial lineup of a cast of hundreds whose records were alive and well as this book went to press.

Zander Hollander and Dave Schulz

BASEBALL

Iron Hoss

NEW YORK, Oct. 27, 1884—Pitching for the third day in a row, as he has done so often during the season, Charley "Hoss" Radbourn hurled his third successive victory in leading the National League champion Providence Grays to a clean sweep in their playoff with the New York Metropolitans, American Association champions.

The sweep climaxed a phenomenal season for Radbourn, in which he won 60 games and lost 12 while Providence was racking up a 84–28 record. Using an overhand delivery which begins with a running start, Radbourn led the league with 441 strikeouts, a 1.38 earned-run average, 73 complete games in 75 starts, and 678⅔ innings pitched. In 15 of the games in which he didn't pitch, he was in the outfield, from where he could be called to the mound if necessary. Substitutions are not allowed, even for pitchers, once the game is under way.

The 29-year-old Radbourn was not even the team's starting pitcher at the beginning of the season, but took over after Charley Sweeney was dismissed for insubordination. Radbourn's success—which included 18 straight victories during one stretch—was not without agonizing effort. When he woke up in the morning, Hoss couldn't even raise his right arm high enough to comb his hair. In order to warm up for a game, he would arrive at the field two hours before the rest of the team and start throwing, his pitches going only a few feet at first. When his teammates arrived, Radbourn would be standing on second base ready to peg the ball home.

Most victories, season: 60, Charles Radbourn, Providence (NL), 1884

Duffy's Day

PITTSBURGH, Pa., Sept. 29, 1894—The hitters have won the battle of the pitching rubber. Pint-sized Hugh Duffy laced two hits today as Boston defeated Pittsburgh, 6–5, and the Beantown centerfielder finished the season with a .438 batting average. The only league-leader to have a higher average was Tip O'Neill, who was credited with a .492 in 1887, the year bases on balls were counted as hits.

Duffy, who stands 5-feet 7-inches and weighs 165 pounds, has always been a good hitter, batting well over .300 each year since he came into the league in 1890. This season he led the National League in hits with 237; doubles with 51; home runs, 18; runs batted in, 143; and slugging, .690. In addition, back on June 18, he tied a major league mark by reaching first base three times in one inning.

Much of the credit for Duffy's success—and that of the other hitters, too—must go to the rule implemented this year that moved the pitchers back to a distance of 60-feet 6-inches from home plate and required the hurlers to work from a 12-inch by 4-inch rubber slab.

Highest batting average, season: .438, Hugh Duffy, Boston (NL), 1894

The Kid Shoots for Seven

BALTIMORE, Md., Sept. 27, 1897—People came from miles around to see the showdown. There were 3,000 men on the rooftops, plus 500 or so who hopped on and off the fences, depending upon the proximity of constables. And inside the ballpark today, 25,390 paid for the privilege of seeing the Bostons and Baltimores battle. Another 1,000 were inside the gates *gratis*, gaining access when a bleacher gate gave way under the crush of the crowd.

The showdown came, as expected, and The Kid won. Charles A. "Kid" Nichols, as nifty a righthander as baseball has seen, picked up his 30th victory of the season, giving him a record seven consecutive 30-win seasons. But what was more important to The Kid was that it was the second time in this three-game series that he had pitched a victory against the Orioles. This gave Boston a game-and-a-half lead over the defending champions in the National League pennant race.

It wasn't one of Nichols's better efforts, although he did extend his record. He gave up 13 hits, three walks, and hit an Oriole as Boston won, 19–10. The Kid had a little offensive punch of his own, getting three hits, including one in the seventh inning when Boston rallied for nine runs and put the game out of reach.

Most seasons 30 or more victories: 7, Charles A. Nichols, Boston (NL), 1891–97

Rubber Arm

CHICAGO, Ill. Oct. 6, 1908—The White Sox called on Ed Walsh for the fourth game in a row, but the big righthander didn't have anything left today as Detroit went on to win the game, 7–0, and clinch the American League pennant.

Walsh, who had a 39–15 record in 66 games this season, came on in relief after Detroit jumped on Guy White in the first inning. Before Walsh could retire the side, Detroit had a 4–0 lead. The 3⅔ innings Walsh pitched raised his season's total to 464, a modern record.

Walsh had pitched Chicago into contention, winning a complete-game victory, 6–1, over Detroit yesterday to pull his team to within one-half game of the Tigers. In the game before that, Walsh recorded his seventh save of the season as he came in with the bases loaded late in the game to preserve a 3–2 victory over Cleveland. Four days ago, also against Cleveland, Walsh pitched a four-hitter, struck out 15, and walked only one, but lost, 1–0, as Addie Joss hurled a perfect no-hit, no-run game against the White Sox.

In addition to innings pitched, games, victories, and saves, Walsh led the AL with 269 strikeouts, 42 complete games, and 11 shutouts.

Most innings pitched, season (since 1900): 464, Edward A. Walsh, Chicago (AL), 1908

Cy Young's Last Game

BROOKLYN, N.Y., Oct. 6, 1911—The Brooklyn Superbas drove Cy Young off the mound and into retirement with an eight-run barrage in the seventh inning of today's game with the Boston Rustlers.

Denton True "Cy" Young, holder of the major league records for both most-games-won and most-games-lost, was touched for eight straight hits and eight runs in the second game of a doubleheader at Washington Park. After Brooklyn's Bob Coulson doubled, Young threw his glove down in disgust and walked off the mound. The Superbas had broken up a 3–3 tie when pinch-hitter Zack Wheat singled home Otto Miller, who had tripled. The floodgates were open and Brooklyn went on to rout the team with the worst record in the National League, 13–3.

Cy Young won 511 games.   *UPI*

Young, 44 years old and fat, finished the year with four wins and five losses in the National League, to go with the 3–4 record he compiled with Cleveland in the AL earlier this season. It was the 315th defeat in his 22-year career, and goes with his 511 victories, both totals unapproached by anyone else. Young is the only man to win 200 or more games in each league, playing with Cleveland and Boston in the American League between 1901 and the middle of this season. He won 222 games during that period. Young broke into the major leagues with Cleveland in 1890, when that city had a National League franchise. He also played with St. Louis in addition to his brief stint with the Rustlers this season.

Before the season even began, Young indicated his desire to quit playing. He was trying to lose weight at Hot Springs, Ark., while avoiding spring training, a ritual he had long detested. It was there that he made his annual retirement announcement. This time he meant it.

Most games started, career: 818, Denton "Cy" Young, Cleveland (NL), 1890–98; St. Louis (NL), 1899–1900; Boston (AL), 1901–08; Cleveland (AL), 1909–11; Boston (NL), 1911

Most complete games, career: 751, Denton "Cy" Young, Cleveland (NL), 1890–98; St. Louis (NL), 1899–1900; Boston (AL), 1901–08; Cleveland (AL), 1909–11; Boston (NL), 1911

Most games won, career: 511, Denton "Cy" Young, Cleveland (NL), 1890–98; St. Louis (NL), 1899–1900; Boston (AL), 1901–08; Cleveland (AL), 1909–11; Boston (NL), 1911

Most games lost, career: 315, Denton "Cy" Young, Cleveland (NL), 1890–98; St. Louis (NL), 1899–1900; Boston (AL), 1901–08; Cleveland (AL), 1909–11; Boston (NL), 1911

Instant Major Leaguers

PHILADELPHIA, Pa., May 18, 1912—The crowd of 20,000 thought the game was a joke, the Philadelphia players loved the batting practice, and pitcher Aloysius Travers worked his way into the record book.

With the regular Detroit players on strike, the team's management faced a stiff fine from the league if nine players were not in uniform for today's game. The major league team that was on the field in Detroit uniforms turned out to be several members of the St. Joseph's College team, other assorted amateurs, and a couple of former big-leaguers on the Detroit executive payroll.

The regular Detroit players had warmed up before the game, then refused to take the field. They were protesting the suspension of Ty Cobb by American League president Ban Johnson after Cobb had climbed into the stands to go at it with a fan who had been riding him particularly hard in New York three days ago.

It took only an hour and 55 minutes for Philadelphia to bang out 25 hits off Travers, score 24 runs, and steal eight bases. The final score was 24–2. Travers, a former star on the St. Joseph's team, went the full eight innings and received little fielding support from his mates, who committed nine errors. Offensively, Detroit managed four hits, which produced the two runs. Each recruit picked up $50 for his efforts.

Most runs allowed by a pitcher, game: 24, Aloysius Travers, Detroit (AL), May 18, 1912

Rube Marquard of the New York Giants won 19 straight games from the start of the 1912 season.   *UPI*

Rube the Great

CHICAGO, Ill., July 8, 1912—He knew it wouldn't last. New York Giant pitcher Rube Marquard had opened the season with a victory over Brooklyn. He won his next game, too. And the one after that. It kept going that way through April, May, and June. Five days ago, on July 3, at the Polo Grounds in New York, Marquard gave up nine hits, five walks, and had to deal with men on base in every inning but one. His teammates worked only four hits off Napoleon Rucker, but the Giants managed to squeak by Brooklyn with a 2–1 victory, giving Rube his 19th consecutive triumph.

He hadn't lost a game and the season was nearly half over. The victory tied him with Tim Keefe of the old New York team who, back in 1888, had the advantage of pitching from much closer to the plate.

Chicago pitcher Jimmy Lavender came into today's duel with Marquard riding a modest streak of his own: 34 consecutive innings of shutout pitching. The Giants ended that string in the third inning, but Lavender had the last laugh as the Cubs scored six runs off Marquard in six innings before the Giant lefty was lifted for a pinch-hitter. Heinie Zimmerman and Joe Tinker led the Chicago attack and the team played errorless ball in support of Lavender. The Cub hurler yielded only five hits as Chicago ended Marquard's skein with a 6–2 victory.

Most consecutive games won, start of season: 19, Richard W. "Rube" Marquard, New York (NL), April 11 to July 3, 1912

Triple Threat

CINCINNATI, Ohio, Oct. 6, 1912—Pittsburgh centerfielder John Owen "Chief" Wilson rapped out a single and a triple to lead a 19-hit attack in a 16–6 victory over Cincinnati. For Wilson, who finished the season with a .304 batting average, the triple was his 36th of the season, an all-time major league record for three-base hits.

The native of Austin, Tex., has been hitting the ball well all season and has used his speed to stretch many a double into a triple. Earlier this year he set a major league record by hitting six triples in five consecutive games between June 17 and June 20.

Most triples, season: 36, J. Owen Wilson, Pittsburgh (NL), 1912
Most triples, five consecutive games: 6, J. Owen Wilson, Pittsburgh (NL), June 17–20, 1912

Pittsburgh's J. Owen "Chief" Wilson hit 36 triples in 1912.   *UPI*

Goose Eggs in the Clutch

PHILADELPHIA, Pa., Oct. 8, 1913—Christy Mathewson singled home the first run of the game today as the New York
Giants went on to beat Philadelphia, 3–0, and tie the World
Series at one game each. The shutout was Mathewson's first in
this series, and with the three he pitched in the 1905 Series
against these same Athletics, it gives him the all-time record of
four shutouts in World Series competition.

In winning today, Mathewson gave up eight hits, walked one,

The New York Giants' Christy Mathewson pitched four World Series
shutouts. *UPI*

struck out five, and was hurt by two errors, one of which almost cost him the shutout.

Amos Strunk led off the ninth with a single and Jack Barry followed with a sacrifice bunt. Larry Doyle made a throwing error on the bunt, and the A's had men on second and third with none out. Hooks Wiltse, substituting for the injured Fred Merkle at first, made a sensational stop of a smash by Johnny Lapp and threw out Strunk at the plate. With Barry on third, pitcher Eddie Plank sizzled another one at Wiltse, who again threw home, and Barry was tagged out in a rundown. Danny Murphy then grounded out, pitcher to first, to end the game.

The 33-year-old Mathewson thus went into the record book again, adding another line to go with his modern NL mark of 37 victories in 1908 and his record of 11 seasons pitching 300 or more innings.

Most games won, season, National League (since 1900): 37, Christy Mathewson, New York (NL), 1908
World Series:
Most shutouts, career: 4, Christy Mathewson, New York (NL), 1905 (3) and 1913 (1)

Streaking Giants

NEW YORK, Sept. 30, 1916—There was good news and bad news for the 38,000 fans who showed up at the Polo Grounds today. The good news was that Rube Benton pitched a one-hitter as the Giants beat Boston, 4–0, to extend their winning streak to 26 games. The bad news was that Boston won the second game of the doubleheader, 8–2, to snap the streak.

The loss came as Rabbit Maranville turned in one fielding gem after another at shortstop in support of George Tyler's pitching in the nightcap. The death knell for the streak was sounded in the seventh inning when the Braves scored five runs. The key blows were back-to-back home runs by Carlisle "Red" Smith and Sherry Magee off the Giants' Slim Sallee.

During the 26-game streak, which began Sept. 7, the Giants beat every other team in the league at least once, although all the games were at home. But despite the string, today's loss eliminated the McGrawmen from any chance of winning the pennant.

Most consecutive victories: 26, New York (NL), Sept. 7–30, 1916

Three-Bag Man

DETROIT, Mich., Sept. 22, 1916—Sam Crawford, the greatest triples-hitter baseball has ever known, stroked the 312th three-bagger of his career today to spark Detroit to a 6–5 victory over Washington.

Though overshadowed by teammate Ty Cobb when it comes to public acclaim, Crawford has had some distinctions, such as being the only man ever to lead each major league in home runs. In addition, the lefthanded-hitting outfielder shares the American League's single-season record for triples with 26, hit in 1914.

Despite his proclivity for hitting triples, Crawford has never hit two in one inning or four in one game, achievements which would have earned him another line in the record book.

A native of Wahoo, Neb., Crawford broke into the majors with Cincinnati in 1899, where he led the National League in home runs in 1901 with 16. He came to Detroit in 1903 and led the AL sluggers with seven home runs in 1908.

Most triples, career: 312, Sam Crawford, Cincinnati (NL), 1899–1902; Detroit (AL), 1903–1917

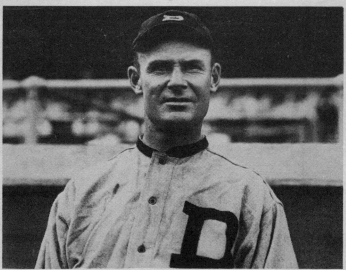

Detroit's Sam "Wahoo" Crawford hit 312 triples in his career.   *UPI*

Mr. 000 000 000

PHILADELPHIA, Pa., Oct. 2, 1916—"Alexander the Great" is what they are calling Grover Cleveland "Pete" Alexander today after the 29-year-old righthander hurled a record 16th shutout for his 33rd victory of the season. Pitching in the hitter's paradise called Baker Bowl, Alexander has had only 11 losses for the Phillies this season.

In today's 2–0 triumph, Pete scattered three singles among Boston hitters and allowed no runner to get past second base, as he gave up no walks and struck out four. A 4–1 loss in the second game of the doubleheader dimmed the record-book performance by Alexander, since it kept Philadelphia one game behind league-leading Brooklyn.

For the purists, Alexander's feat is only a modern record, since back in 1876 George Bradley is credited with 16 shutouts for St. Louis. But he was pitching from the old 50-foot distance rather than the modern 60-foot 6-inch range.

Most shutouts, season: 16, Grover C. Alexander, Philadelphia (NL), 1916

Babe on the Mound

BOSTON, Mass., Oct. 9, 1916—Boston pitcher George "Babe" Ruth gave up a first-inning home run to Hi Myers and held Brooklyn to only six hits in 14 innings as Boston took a 2–0 lead in the World Series with a 2–1 triumph here today. In going the distance, Ruth established a record for most innings pitched in a World Series game.

Ruth struck out three and walked three as Brooklyn left five men on base. This was the first Series victory for the lefthanded Ruth, who compiled a 23–12 record during the regular season while leading the American League with nine shutouts and a 1.75 earned-run average, a record low for a lefthanded pitcher.

World Series:
Most innings pitched, game: 14, George H. "Babe" Ruth, Boston (AL), Oct. 9, 1916

Babe Ruth of the Boston Red Sox pitched more innings in a World
Series game than anyone else.   *UPI*

On and On and On and On and

BOSTON, Mass., May 1, 1920—Communist-inspired May Day riots were the rule of the day in most major cities (three persons were killed in riots in Paris), but here in Boston the activity was much more restrained. For a record 26 innings, the Brooklyn Robins and Boston Braves sparred in an effort to win a baseball game before a chilled crowd of about 2,000. When it became too dark to play, the score was still tied, 1–1, as it had been at the end of every inning since the sixth.

Pitchers Joe Oeschger for Boston and Leon Cadore for Brooklyn went the entire distance, with Oeschger having somewhat the better of it by allowing only nine hits, including one that led to a Brooklyn run in the fifth inning. The Braves rapped 15 hits off Cadore, but could pick up only one run, in the home half of the sixth.

Only twice did it look as though the game might have a decisive outcome. In the ninth, Boston filled the bases with one out, but Charlie Pick grounded to Ivy Olson, who tagged Ray Powell on the basepath and threw to first in time to double the batter. End of threat.

Leon Cadore of the Brooklyn Robins went the distance in baseball's longest game.   *UPI*

Joe Oeschger was the Boston Braves' pitcher in the marathon game. *UPI*

Boston had a scare in the 17th inning when Oeschger allowed two hits in one inning for the only time in the game. The bases were full of Robins when Rowdy Elliot knocked the ball back to the mound. Oeschger threw home to force Zack Wheat, but the relay to first was fumbled by Walt Holke. The first baseman retrieved the ball and whipped it home in time for catcher Hank Gowdy to tag Ed Konetchy, trying to score from second on the play.

Most innings pitched, game: 26, Leon J. Cadore, Brooklyn (NL), May 1, 1920, and Joseph C. Oeschger, Boston (NL), May 1, 1920
Most batsmen faced, game: 97, Leon J. Cadore, Brooklyn (NL), May 1, 1920
Longest game in innings: 26, Brooklyn vs. Boston (NL), May 1, 1920

17

George Sisler of the St. Louis Browns rapped 257 hits in one season.

Sizzling Sisler

ST. LOUIS, Mo., Oct. 3, 1920—George Sisler won the battle of St. Louis today, battering the scandal-scarred Chicago White Sox for three hits in a 16–7 victory for the Browns.

Sisler, the former University of Michigan athlete, showed he was as adroit with the bat as he is with a glove, finishing the season with a record 257 hits and a .407 batting average. He was also among the leading fielders in the league, topping them all in assists by a first baseman.

Sisler far outdistanced the National League's leading batter, Rogers Hornsby of the crosstown Cardinals, who wound up hitting .370 for the season. Playing in 154 games, Sisler scored 137 runs this season in 631 times at bat.

Revelations of the 1919 World Series scandal came out this year, and were followed by charges that some White Sox players had dumped this season's pennant. But the way they played today it didn't look as though the White Sox were good enough to throw anything, as the Browns pounded out 18 hits in the assault.

Most hits, one season: 257, George H. Sisler, St. Louis (AL), 1920

Boom-Boom Bottomley

BROOKLYN, N.Y., Sept. 16, 1924—Brooklyn's pennant express was ambushed today as Jim Bottomley rapped six hits—including home runs in two consecutive times at bat—and drove in a major league record 12 runs. Bottomley also scored another run, thus having a direct hand in 13 of the 17 St. Louis runs in the Cardinals' 17–3 victory.

Bottomley treated five Brooklyn pitchers with equal disdain, getting at least one hit off each. Sunny Jim started his barrage with a bases-loaded single off Rube Ehrhardt in the first inning, driving in two runs. He doubled home a run in the next inning before belting a grand-slam home run in the fourth, to make the score 9–1. Next time up, in the sixth, he socked a two-run blast, followed by a two-run single in the seventh. Bottomley ended the day's work by singling home Rogers Hornsby in the ninth inning for the final St. Louis tally.

The Brooklyn rooters were of course dismayed, but none as much as Wilbert Robertson, who was in the crowd of 20,000.

Robertson had set the old record of 11 runs batted in with the Baltimore Orioles in 1892 against, you guessed it, St. Louis.

Most runs batted in, game: 12, James L. Bottomley, St. Louis (NL), Sept. 16, 1924

End of the Line

WASHINGTON, D.C., Sept. 21, 1927—The Big Train made his last stop today, running out of smoke in the fourth inning against the St. Louis Browns. If Walter Johnson's fastball wasn't what it once was, his competitive spirit remained intact.

Washington's Walter Johnson struck out 3,508 and notched 113 shutouts. *UPI*

Recovering from a broken leg sustained in spring training, Johnson worked hard to achieve a 5–5 record in his final season. Today's game didn't figure in it, since Washington came back to win, 10–7, after Walter left the mound with one out in the fourth inning. He also missed a chance to add to his record total of 113 career shutouts. But Johnson did strike out two Browns, to raise his major league record total to 3,508.

Johnson came into the major leagues after earning a reputation in the semipro Snake River Valley League, striking out 166 batters in 11 games as a teenager. He went directly to Washington, and, disdaining the overhand pitching style favored by most speedballers, showed he could throw smoke from a motion somewhere between sidearm and three-quarter arm delivery.

Despite his brilliance, Johnson was surrounded by mediocrity and he didn't play in a World Series until 1924, well past his prime, at the age of 36. His effectiveness was not just in his blazing fastball, but in his control, too. In 1913, perhaps his best year, the Big Train won 36, lost only 7, and walked only 38 men all season in compiling an earned-run average of 1.14, a record for a right-handed pitcher.

Most strikeouts, American League, career: 3,508. Walter Johnson, Washington (AL), 1907–27.

Most shutouts, career: 113, Walter Johnson, Washington (AL), 1907–27

Most American League games started: 666, Walter Johnson, Washington, 1907–27

Most shutouts lost, career: 65, Walter Johnson, Washington (AL), 1907–27

Most consecutive seasons pitching for one team: 21, Walter Johnson, Washington (AL), 1907–27

Most American League games won: 416, Walter Johnson, Washington, 1907–27

Most American League games lost: 279, Walter Johnson, Washington, 1907–27

Most innings pitched, one league: 5,924, Walter Johnson, Washington (AL), 1907–27

Most hit batsmen, career: 205, Walter Johnson, Washington (AL), 1907–27

Most batters faced, one league, career: 23,200, Walter Johnson, Washington (AL), 1907–27

Most wild pitches, American League, career: 156, Walter Johnson, Washington, 1907–27

Ty Cobb ended his career with a .367 batting average.   *UPI*

Cobb's Corner

NEW YORK, Sept. 11, 1928—A crowd of 50,000 was on hand
in Yankee Stadium to see an historic moment in baseball. They
watched the defending World Champion New York Yankees
defeat Philadelphia, 5–3, and extend their lead to 2½ games
over the Athletics. The margin of victory was provided in the
bottom of the eighth inning when, with Lou Gehrig on second,
Babe Ruth smashed a home run off Lefty Grove.

But the historic moment came in the top of the ninth inning
when Ty Cobb was sent up to pinch-hit for third baseman
Jimmy Dykes. The 42-year-old Georgia Peach popped a fly ball
past third that was gathered in by shortstop Mark Koenig. It
was Ty Cobb's last time at bat in the major leagues.

The inauspicious swan song didn't damage Cobb's average
very much, for he had 114 hits in 353 times at bat this season for
a healthy .323 average. And it in no way diminished his career
totals, which included a record .367 lifetime batting average,
only one of his many major league marks.

Highest batting average, career: .367, Tyrus R. Cobb, Detroit (AL),
1905–26, Philadelphia (AL), 1927–28

Most seasons leading major leagues in batting: 11, Tyrus R. Cobb, Detroit (AL), 1907, 1909–15, 1917–19

Most consecutive seasons leading major leagues in batting: 7, Tyrus R. Cobb, Detroit (AL), 1909–15

Most seasons batting .300 or better: 23, Tyrus R. Cobb, Detroit (AL), 1905–26, Philadelphia (AL), 1927–28

Most plate appearances, American League, career: 12,713, Tyrus R. Cobb, Detroit (AL), 1905–26, Philadelphia (AL), 1927–28

Most seasons leading major league in hits: 7, Tyrus R. Cobb, Detroit (AL), 1907, 1909, 1911–12, 1915–17, 1919

Most hits, American League, career: 4,191, Tyrus R. Cobb, Detroit (AL), 1905–26, Philadelphia (AL), 1927–28

Most games, five or more hits: 14, Tyrus R. Cobb, Detroit (AL), 1905–26, Philadelphia (AL), 1927–28

Most singles, American League, career (since 1900): 892, Tyrus R. Cobb, Detroit (AL), 1905–26, Philadelphia (AL), 1927–28

Most times stolen home: 35 Tyrus R. Cobb, Detroit (AL), 1905–26, Philadelphia (AL), 1927–28

Ruthian Feat

ST. LOUIS, Mo., Oct. 9, 1928—Playing hurt and to the accompaniment of boos, hisses, jeers, and a few bottles from the leftfield stands, Babe Ruth continued his torrid hitting and swatted three home runs today to lead the New York Yankees to a 7–3 World Series victory over St. Louis.

The home runs accounted for Ruth's only runs batted in during the Series as the Yankees swept all four games. Ruth's 10 hits in 16 times at bat gave him a record .625 batting average. The Cardinal pitchers—Billy Sherdel, Grover Cleveland "Pete" Alexander, Jesse Haines, Syl Johnson—could do nothing with the Babe as the Yankees won the first two games in New York, 4–1 and 9–3, before taking the pair here by identical 7–3 scores.

Ruth's three home runs, the second time he has accomplished this feat in a World Series game, helped the Yanks to a team-record nine for the Series. Lou Gehrig, who also clouted a circuit blast today, had four round-trippers in the Series, tying the Babe's 1926 mark. Thanks to the Bambino being on base so often, Gehrig, who followed him in the batting order, drove in nine runs, a record for a four-game series.

Ruth played the entire Series with a bum knee, but the injury didn't prevent him from bringing the caterwauling fans in the stands to near silence when he made a spectacular one-handed, knee-sliding grab of a fly ball to end the game and the Series.

Hack Performance

CHICAGO, Ill., Sept. 28, 1930—In an era when American Leaguers are dominating the hitting statistics, Chicago Cub centerfielder Lewis "Hack" Wilson drove in two runs with a pair of singles in today's season finale to push his RBI total to a record 190 for the season as the Cubs outslugged Cincinnati, 13–11. In yesterday's game, Wilson smacked his fifty-fifth and fifty-sixth home runs of the season to establish a National League record.

   Nicknamed for the popular strongman and wrestler, Hackenschmidt, Wilson is a stocky, broadfaced, no-neck righthanded batter who can hit with power. This season is the fourth time in five years that he has led the NL in home runs, and the second straight season he has driven in more than 180 runs, the only player in senior circuit history to accomplish this.

Most runs batted in, season: 190, Lewis R. "Hack" Wilson, Chicago (NL), 1930

Fence Busters

CHICAGO, Ill., Oct. 2, 1932—Murderers Row did it again, establishing offensive records left and right as the New York Yankees won their 12th consecutive World Series game today, downing the Chicago Cubs, 13–6.

   As in 1927 and 1928, the Yanks were led by Babe Ruth and Lou Gehrig in sweeping their National League foes in four games. New York's team batting average of .313 is a record for a four-game series, as was Chicago's .253 for a losing team.

   In addition to the team records, there were some distinctive individual performances. In yesterday's third game, for example, as Babe Ruth strode up to the plate in the fifth inning, a lemon rolled across his path. Glaring at pitcher Charlie Root,

Lou Gehrig congratulates Babe Ruth in the Yankees' record-smashing 1932 World Series.
UPI

Ruth took two balls and two strikes, pointing after each pitch to a spot over the right field fence where he intended to hit the ball. The Babe was off in his prediction, however, as the ball sailed over the fence in dead center. Also in yesterday's game, Yankee pitcher George Pipgras struck out a record five times in five plate appearances, while the Yanks were winning, 7–5.

In today's finale, Lou Gehrig scored twice, each time on a Tony Lazzeri home run, to tie Babe Ruth's record for nine runs scored in a four-game series.

Some of the other marks established for a four-game series were one- and two-team records for times at bat, runs, hits, total bases, singles, home runs, runs batted in, walks and hit batsmen. The big hitters for the Cubs were Riggs Stephenson, Frank Demaree, Kiki Cuyler, Charlie Grimm, and Billy Herman.

World Series:
Most runs, individual, four-game series: 9, Lou Gehrig, New York (AL), 1932 (Ties George H. "Babe" Ruth, New York (AL), 1928)
Highest slugging average, both teams: .459, New York (AL) and Chicago (NL), 1932
Most series batting .300 or higher: 6, George H. "Babe" Ruth, New York (AL), 1921, 1923, 1926, 1928, 1932
Most strikeouts, batter, one game: 5, George Pipgras, New York (AL), Oct. 1, 1932

The Bambino Bows Out

BOSTON, Mass., June 2, 1935—As dramatic off the field as he is flamboyant on it, Babe Ruth precipitated a controversy that ended in his unconditional release today from the Boston Braves. Team president Judge Emil F. Fuchs made the decision after Ruth had attended a shipboard party in violation of curfew regulations set by manager Bill McKechnie.

The 41-year-old Ruth had been nothing more than a drawing card for the hapless Braves, wallowing in the National League cellar. Other teams in the league were holding "Babe Ruth Days" in an effort to boost attendance. A chronic knee injury had reduced the Bambino's playing time and in his last game, May 30, in Philadelphia, he played left field only briefly and failed to get a hit in his one time at bat. The day before, he settled for a pair of walks. But only a week ago, Ruth showed he was still capable of destroying pitchers.

Playing at Forbes Field in Pittsburgh, the Babe smashed three home runs off Pirate hurlers Red Lucas and Guy Bush. They were the 712th, 713th, and 714th home runs of his career, which began as a lefthanded pitcher with the Boston Red Sox in 1914.

The Sultan of Swat, Il Bambino, the Babe, or George Herman Ruth, they all started out in Baltimore, where as a seven-year-old street urchin he was sent to St. Mary's Industrial Home. He never lost the rough edge of his origins, although he won the hearts and respect of America. An early Boston teammate, Harry Hooper, recalled, "Sometimes I still can't believe

This was the Babe in his heyday with the Yankees.   *UPI*

what I saw, this 19-year-old kid, crude, poorly educated . . . gradually transformed into the idol of American youth and the symbol of baseball the world over."

27

Highest slugging average, lifetime: .692, George H. "Babe" Ruth, Boston (AL), 1914–19; New York (AL), 1920–34; Boston (NL), 1935

Most bases on balls, lifetime: 2,056, George H. "Babe" Ruth, Boston (AL), 1914–19; New York (AL), 1920–34; Boston (NL), 1935

Most seasons, 50 or more home runs: 4, George H. "Babe" Ruth, New York (AL), 1920–21, 1927–28

Most seasons 40 or more home runs: 11, George H. "Babe" Ruth, New York (AL), 1920–21, 1923–24, 1926–34

Most seasons leading major leagues in home runs: 11, George H. "Babe" Ruth, Boston (AL), 1918–19, New York (AL), 1920–21, 1923–24, 1926–29, 1931

Most seasons leading major leagues in runs scored: 8, George H. "Babe" Ruth, Boston (AL), 1919; New York (AL), 1920–21, 1923–24, 1926–28

Most seasons leading major leagues in runs batted in: 5, George H. "Babe" Ruth, New York (AL), 1920–21, 1923, 1926, 1928

Lefty Is Right

WASHINGTON, D.C., July 7, 1937—Vernon "Lefty" Gomez, pitching for the fourth time in the five All-Star Games that have been played, did the hurling and Yankee teammate Lou

Starters in the 1937 All-Star Game: Vernon "Lefty" Gomez (left) and Dizzy Dean.   *UPI*

Gehrig did the hitting as the American League beat the Nationals, 8–3, before a crowd of 31,391 that included President Franklin Roosevelt in Griffith Stadium. The victory was credited to Gomez, a record third time he has been the winning pitcher in the All-Star Game.

With Gehrig driving in four runs on a homer and a double, Gomez kept the NL at bay by allowing only one hit and walking none in his three-inning stint as starting pitcher. In 1935, Lefty worked a record six innings in the All-Star Game and allowed only three hits as the AL won, 4–1, in Cleveland. Gomez was also the winning pitcher in the first All-Star Game in 1933, which the AL won, 4–2, in Chicago.

National League starter Dizzy Dean accepted the blame for today's loss. "I shook [Gabby] Hartnett off twice and I was belted each time," Dean lamented after the game. One of those belts was a Gehrig home run that opened the AL scoring.

All-Star Game:
Most games won, lifetime: 3, Vernon "Lefty" Gomez, New York (AL), 1933, 1935, 1937

Tiger, Tiger Hitting Right

DETROIT, Mich., Aug. 31, 1937—Rudy York, who was sent down to the minors in June, hit his 29th and 30th home runs of the season today as the Tigers overpowered Washington, 12–3, at Navin Field.

For York, a rookie who played catcher today, the home runs brought his total for the month of August to 18, breaking by one Babe Ruth's mark of 17 homers in a calendar month, September, 1927, the year the Bambino hit 60.

In addition to the long blasts, both off Pete Appleton, York had two singles in a perfect 4-for-4 day. He drove in seven of the Tigers' 12 runs. Back on June 7, York, who was getting his second chance in the big leagues after playing briefly in 1934, had been optioned on 24-hour recall to the Toledo Mud Hens of the American Association as the Tigers called up centerfielder Chet Laabs.

Most home runs in a calendar month: 18, Rudy York, Detroit (AL), August, 1937

Detroit's Rudy York hit 18 homers in one calendar month.   *UPI*

Dutch Treat

BROOKLYN, N.Y., June 15, 1938—There was a festive mood at Ebbets Field as a crowd of 38,748 paid to see the first major league night baseball game in the New York metropolitan area. In the stands were about 500 people from Midland Park, N.J., hometown of Johnny Vander Meer, who had pitched a no-hitter five days ago for the Cincinnati Reds against the Boston Bees.

Tonight, John's parents, his Dutch uncles and aunts and friends were on hand to present him with a gift and to watch the 23-year-old fireballer pitch against the Brooklyn Dodgers. And pitch he did. For six innings, not one Dodger got on base. Then, in the seventh inning, something went wrong and Vander

Cincinnati's Johnny Vander Meer is the only man in history to pitch back-to-back no-hitters. *UPI*

Meer issued consecutive walks to Cookie Lavagetto and Dolph Camilli. He escaped from the inning without giving up a hit, though, and sailed through the eighth. That was 17⅓ consecutive innings of hitless pitching, topped only by the legendary Cy Young's 23 hitless frames in 1904.

With the Reds comfortably ahead, 6–0, Buddy Hassett led off the home half of the last inning by tapping the ball toward the mound. Vandy picked it up and tagged the runner on his way to first. One out. Babe Phelps was up next and walked. Vandy's fastball had gone haywire, for he walked Lavagetto and Camilli again in quick succession. Bases loaded, one out. Ernie Koy came up to bat and drove a hard grounder to Lew Riggs at third. Riggs was so careful fielding the ball and getting it to catcher Ernie Lombardi for the force play that there was no time for a relay and possible double play.

The bases were still full when Leo Durocher came to the plate. A deathly silence filled Ebbets Field. Durocher swung, the crowd groaned, and a hard-hit ball curved foul into the right field stands. Durocher then lofted a short fly to centerfield which Harry Craft hauled in. Vandy had his second no-hitter in five days.

Others had pitched two no-hitters, but none had ever pitched two in one season, much less in successive games.

Most consecutive no-hitters: 2, Johnny Vander Meer, Cincinnati (NL), June 11 and June 15, 1938

Foxx Trot

ST. LOUIS, Mo., June 16, 1938—Question: How can a batter get on base six times, score two runs, and not have a time at bat?

Answer: Ask Jimmy Foxx.

Foxx, leading the American league with 19 home runs and 71 runs batted in, was issued a base on balls in each of his six plate appearances today as the Red Sox beat the St. Louis Browns, 12–8. The Boston first baseman got the passes from three St. Louis hurlers: Les Tietje, Ed Linke, and Russ Van Atta.

The six walks broke the modern mark of five in one game shared by Mel Ott of the New York Giants and Max Bishop of

Red Sox slugger Jimmy Foxx once drews six bases on balls in one game.

the Philadelphia Athletics. It also tied the pre-1900 mark of six walks set by Walter Wilmut of the Chicago Cubs in 1891.

The six plate appearances with no official time at bat duplicated the feat of Miller Huggins with the St. Louis Cardinals in 1910 and Bill Urbanski with the Boston Braves in 1934. These men did it with four walks and two sacrifices, while Charles Smith of Boston received five walks and was hit by a pitched ball back in 1890.

Most walks, game: 6, Jimmy Foxx, Boston (AL), June 16, 1938

All-Star Hitter

CINCINNATI, Ohio, July 6, 1938—Three National League pitchers held the American League to a lone run as the senior circuit All-Stars won the midsummer classic, 4–1, before a crowd of 27,067 in Crosley Field here today.

One of the seven hits given up by the Reds' Johnny Vander Meer, the Cubs' Bill Lee, and Pittsburgh's Mace Brown, went to Charlie Gehringer. The Detroit second baseman, who was 1-for-3 in the game, picked up his tenth All-Star hit in 20 times at bat for a record .500 batting average.

The loss, only the second in six games for the AL, was the first in All-Star competition for Vernon "Lefty" Gomez of the Yankees, who had won three of the previous encounters.

All-Star Game:
Highest batting average (minimum 20 at-bats): .500, Charlie Gehringer, Detroit (AL), 1933–38

Thank You, Mr. Pipp

DETROIT, Mich., May 2, 1939—Batting an anemic .143 with four singles in 28 times at bat, Lou Gehrig benched himself today and thus ended the longest streak of consecutive games played in baseball history, 2,130. Gehrig was replaced by Ellsworth "Babe" Dahlgren, who hit a home run and a double as the Yankees overwhelmed the Tigers, 22–2, at Briggs Stadium.

Gehrig's decision to take himself out of the lineup was made with the approval of manager Joe McCarthy. "He'd let me go until the cows come home," Gehrig said of McCarthy. "He is that considerate of my feelings, but I knew in Sunday's game that I should get out of there." On Sunday, Gehrig was held hitless by Joe Krakauskas and Alex Carresquel as Washington beat New York, 3–2.

"It's tough to see your mates on base, have a chance to win a ball game and not be able to do anything about it," Gehrig said.

Gehrig's streak began June 1, 1925, when he was sent up to pinch-hit for shortstop PeeWee Wanninger. He failed to get a hit off Walter Johnson, but was in the Yankee starting lineup the following day when regular first baseman Wally Pipp told manager Miller Huggins, "I don't feel like getting in there."

Most consecutive games played: 2,130, Lou Gehrig, New York (AL), June 1, 1925 to April 30, 1939

Lou Gehrig, with Yankee manager Joe McCarthy (right), benched himself after 2,130 consecutive games. *UPI*

Yankee clipper Joe DiMaggio hit safely in 56 consecutive games.   *UPI*

Streaking Clipper

CLEVELAND, Ohio, July 17, 1941—A crowd of 67,468, the largest ever to see a major league baseball game played at night, was on hand in Municipal Stadium tonight to see whether Joe DiMaggio could extend his all-time record consecutive-game hitting streak.

The Yankee Clipper hit safely in his 56th straight game yesterday when he smashed Al Milnar's first pitch to him in the first inning through the box for a single. DiMaggio added another single and a double in New York's 10–3 victory over the Indians.

The hitting streak began May 15 in Yankee Stadium in New York when Joltin' Joe went 1-for-4 against the White Sox. When the skein hit 45, DiMaggio eclipsed the former record of 44 set by Wee Willie Keeler of the Baltimore Orioles in 1897.

DiMaggio, who hit in 61 straight games playing in his native San Francisco with the Seals in the Pacific Coast League eight years ago, made four trips to the plate tonight. In the first inning he hit a hard smash that third baseman Ken Keltner knocked down and threw to first in time to get DiMaggio. The next time up Joe walked. After that he hit another drive that Keltner handled.

The bases were full in the eighth when DiMaggio came up to face righthanded Jim Bagby, pitching in relief of lefty Al Smith. DiMag hit a 1-1 pitch on the ground and the hit was turned into a double play that ended the inning as well as his batting streak. The Yankees won, 4–3, but DiMaggio's streak was stopped after 56 games.

Most consecutive games one or more hits: 56, Joe DiMaggio, New York (AL), May 15, 1941, to July 16, 1941

Indian Courage

CLEVELAND, Ohio, July 13, 1954—Al Rosen told American League manager Casey Stengel before today's All-Star Game that he was willing to be dropped from the starting lineup, selected by a poll of the fans. Rosen broke a finger May 25 and the injury had been affecting his performance, but Stengel left the Cleveland infielder in the order, batting fifth and playing first base. Rosen responded by leading the AL to an 11–9 victory, giving Stengel his first victory as an All-Star manager over rookie NL pilot Walter Alston of the Brooklyn Dodgers.

Playing before a crowd of 68,751 in Municipal Stadium, three Indians treated the hometown fans to outstanding performances. Rosen hit two home runs and drove in five runs, Larry Doby clouted a pinch-hit home run and Bobby Avila went 3-for-3 and scored a run. Rosen's five runs batted in tied an All-Star record set by Ted Williams in 1946, and his two homers equaled the efforts of Williams and Pittsburgh's Arky Vaughn in 1941. Despite the bum finger, Rosen played the entire game, eight innings at first before moving to third base, replacing Detroit's Ray Boone, whose homer had provided the margin of victory for the junior circuit.

Special Delivery

NEW YORK, Oct. 8, 1956—Using a no-windup delivery, Don Larsen of the New York Yankees retired 27 Brooklyn Dodger batters in succession today as he pitched the only perfect game in World Series history. There had never even been a no-hitter in the Series, much less a perfect game.

The 27-year-old righthander, a native of Michigan City, Ind., who grew up in San Diego, Cal., retired the final batter, pinch-hitter Dale Mitchell, with a fastball that was called strike three by umpire Babe Pinelli. The Yankees won, 2–0.

Crediting his unusual pitching motion, which is a modification of the stretch pitchers normally use with runners on base, Larsen said after the game, "It gives me better control, it takes nothing off my fastball, and it keeps the batters tense. They have to be ready every second."

There were only four near-hits Dodger batters could manage against the 6-foot 4-inch, 220-pound Larsen, who won only

The Yankees' Don Larsen makes the final pitch in his perfect game against the Dodgers.
UPI

three games while losing 21 two seasons ago before being traded from Baltimore to the Yanks. In the second inning, third baseman Andy Carey got his glove in the way of a liner off the bat of Jackie Robinson. The ball bounced to shortstop Gil MacDougald and he pegged to first in time to nip the fleet Robinson.

In the fifth inning, Mickey Mantle made a spectacular catch in deep left center on a clout by Gil Hodges. The next batter, Sandy Amoros, hit a long drive down the rightfield line that curved foul just before going into the stands. And in the eighth inning, it was Hodges again who almost ruined Larsen's effort when he hit a low smash down the third-base line. Carey made a diving stab, but just to make sure he wasn't called for trapping it, Carey threw to first baseman Joe Collins for an unnecessary putout.

World Series:
Most consecutive batters retired, game: 27, Don Larsen, New York (AL), vs. Brooklyn (NL), Oct. 8, 1956

Splendid Splinter

WASHINGTON, D.C., July 10, 1956—Boston's Ted Williams and the New York Yankees' Mickey Mantle socked consecutive home runs and knocked Warren Spahn out of the box, but it still was not enough to bring victory to the American League today, as the National League won, 7–3, for the sixth time in the last seven All-Star Games.

Williams, the Splendid Splinter who has been playing in these midsummer classics since 1940 when he hasn't been fighting in wars, homered with Chicago's Nellie Fox on base. It was Williams's first All-Star home run in 10 years. His last came in 1946 when he had a pair at Fenway Park in Boston. But the runs batted in today increased his total in All-Star Games to a record 12.

All-Star Game:
Most runs batted in, career: 12, Ted Williams, Boston (AL), 1940–56

The Red Sox' Ted Williams holds the All-Star Game mark of 12 runs batted in.   *UPI*

Pittsburgh's Harvey Haddix retired 36 batters in a row in one game and lost.   *UPI*

12/13ths Perfect

MILWAUKEE, Wis., May 26, 1959—A perfect game that wasn't and a home run that was a double spelled victory for the Milwaukee Braves tonight. Pittsburgh's Harvey "The Kitten" Haddix stymied the heavy-hitting Braves, retiring a record 36 consecutive batters in 12 innings. And although Milwaukee's Lew Burdette gave up 12 hits, the Pirates failed to score in their 13 turns at bat.

Haddix, who struck out eight Braves, started the bottom of the 13th facing Felix Mantilla, who was safe on an error by third baseman Don Hoak. Haddix's perfect game was gone, but it was still better than the 33 consecutive batters retired by Brooklyn's Ed Kimber against Toledo in 1884, back when the American Association was a major league. And even if Haddix's perfect game was ruined, he still had a no-hitter going.

Eddie Mathews sacrificed Mantilla to second. Henry Aaron, leading the majors with a .442 batting average, was walked intentionally. This pitted lefthanded Haddix against righthanded batter Joe Adcock. The big Louisianan teed off on Haddix and parked the ball over the right-centerfield fence. Haddix was dejected, Adcock elated with the home run and the Braves' 3–0 victory, until Frank Dascoli changed the scoring. The umpire said that Aaron, who had cut across the infield after touching second base, had been passed on the baselines by Adcock, so Adcock was out. Aaron then went back, retraced his steps from second, touched third and home to score. He and Mantilla had scored the runs and the Braves won, 2–0. Adcock was given credit for a double. Haddix lost the perfect game, the no-hitter, and picked up a spectacular one-hit loss.

Most consecutive batters retired, game: 36, Harvey Haddix, Pittsburgh (NL), May 26, 1959

Men for All Ages

NEW YORK, July 13, 1960—One man many people consider too young was nominated for one job while another man who is called too old by some got a different job done today.

In Los Angeles, 43-year-old John F. Kennedy won the Democratic nomination for President, while here in Yankee Stadium 39-year-old Stan Musial hit a record sixth home run in All-Star competition to help the National League to a 6–0 victory.

Musial, who laced a pinch-hit single in this year's first All-Star Game, which the NL won, 5–3, in Kansas City two days ago, appeared again in a pinch-hitting role in the second All-Star Game of 1960. Playing in his 19th classic, Stan the Man came up in the fourth inning to bat for pitcher Stan Williams and knocked a solo blast off Gerry Staley for the Nationals' fourth run. All of the runs were scored via homers, one each by San Francisco's Willie Mays, Milwaukee's Eddie Mathews, and Musial's Cardinal teammate, Ken Boyer.

Another old-timer who was roundly cheered by the crowd was Ted Williams, six weeks short of his 42nd birthday, who singled in a pinch-hitting role for the AL.

All-Star Game:
Most home runs, career: 6, Stan Musial, St. Louis (NL), 1948–60

The Cardinals' Stan Musial hit six All-Star Game home runs. *UPI*

Driving Them In

PITTSBURGH, Pa., Oct. 12, 1960—Yankee second baseman Bobby Richardson—described by sportswriters as too good to be true—was almost too good to be believed again today as he touched Pirate pitchers for a pair of triples, drove in three runs, earned another line in the record book and, incidentally, helped New York to a 12–0 World Series triumph.

Richardson, a native of South Carolina who doesn't smoke, drink, or cuss, set a single-game record with six runs batted in during the third game of the Series, won by the Yankees, 10–0. The 25-year-old, 5-foot 9-inch, 165-pound Richardson slammed a bases-loaded home run in the first inning of that game, went 4-for-4 at the plate, and drove in two more runs to eclipse the mark of five RBIs shared by Yankees Bill Dickey and Tony

Lazzeri, set in 1936 and equaled by Mickey Mantle in the opening game of this Series.

Today, Richardson tripled in the third inning off Tom Cheney to drive in Johnny Blanchard and Yogi Berra. These were his 10th and 11th runs batted in, surpassing the 10 RBIs by Berra in 1956 and duplicated by Ted Kluszewski of the White Sox in last year's Series. Bobby upped the record to 12 when he tripled again in the seventh inning off Clem Labine, scoring Blanchard.

World Series:
Most runs batted in, series: 12, Bobby Richardson, New York (AL), 1960
Most runs batted in, game: 6, Bobby Richardson, New York (AL), Oct. 8, 1960

One Up on the Babe

NEW YORK, Oct. 1, 1961—The record that many people didn't want to see broken was broken today as New York's Roger Maris hit his 61st home run in the final game of the season off Boston Red Sox rookie Tracy Stallard. It was the 27-year-old lefthanded batter's 49th home run off a righthanded pitcher and his 30th in Yankee Stadium as he pulled a waist-high fastball on a two-strike count over the rightfield fence in the fourth inning.

Earlier in the season, baseball Commissioner Ford Frick said if Maris were to break Babe Ruth's record of 60 home runs— the Babe hit his 60th on the final day of the 1927 season—it would be noted in the record book with an asterisk. Frick said the difference was that Ruth played a 154-game schedule while Maris's Yankees had a 162-game schedule. Nevertheless, the two home run hitters had almost the same number of plate appearances in their record-breaking season, Ruth 692 and Maris 698. After 154 games this season, Maris had hit 59 home runs.

A crowd of 23,154 was on hand to see Maris, a native of Fargo, N.D., give the Yankees a 1–0 victory over Boston.

Most home runs, season: 61, Roger Maris, New York (AL), 1961

The Yankees' Roger Maris belts his 61st homer against the Red Sox.

Yogi's String

LOS ANGELES, Cal., Oct. 5, 1963—Lawrence Peter Berra had as much trouble hitting Don Drysdale as did his Yankee teammates and as a result the Los Angeles Dodgers won their third straight World Series game today, 1–0.

Berra, who has carried his childhood nickname of Yogi

throughout his baseball life, was sent up to pinch-hit for pitcher Jim Bouton. Berra failed to get a hit, but his appearance extended many of his World Series records. This marked the 14th time Yogi has been in a World Series, all with the Yankees. In 75 games, he has had 259 times at bat, with 71 hits, 49 of them singles, all record totals. In addition, Berra has handled more chances and completed more putouts than any fielder at any position in World Series history.

World Series:

Most World Series: 14, L.P. "Yogi" Berra, New York (AL), 1949–53, 1955–58, 1960–63

Most games: 75, L.P. "Yogi" Berra, New York (AL), 1949–53, 1955–58, 1960–63

Most times at bat: 259, L.P. "Yogi" Berra, New York (AL), 1949–53, 1955–58, 1960–63

Most hits: 71, L.P. "Yogi" Berra, New York (AL), 1949–53, 1955–58, 1960–63

Most singles: 49, L.P. "Yogi" Berra, New York (AL), 1949–53, 1955–58, 1960–63

Most chances accepted, catcher: 457, L.P. "Yogi" Berra, New York (AL), 1949–53, 1955–58, 1960–63

Most putouts, catcher: 421, L.P. "Yogi" Berra, New York (AL), 1949–53, 1955–58, 1960–63

The Yankees' Yogi Berra pinch-hits against the Dodgers in his 259th World Series at-bat. *UPI*

Changing of the Guard

ST. LOUIS, Mo., Oct. 15, 1964—Upheavals were the order of the day today. On the banks of the Moscow River a couple of guys named Brezhnev and Kosygin toppled Nikita Khruschev from power in the Soviet Union. And on the banks of the Mississippi, a couple of guys named Gibson and Brock ended the World Series reign of Mickey Mantle, Whitey Ford, and the New York Yankees.

With Bob Gibson pitching and Lou Brock hitting and stealing bases, the St. Louis Cardinals beat New York, 7–5, in the seventh and final game of the World Series here today. The game marked the last post-season appearances of Ford, a part-time pitching coach, who developed a sore arm in losing the opening game of the Series, and Mantle, who hit three home runs, scored eight runs, drove in eight runs, and batted .333 for the Series. Between them, they accounted for numerous records.

It was the second successive World Series loss for the Yankees. Only in 1921 and 1922, in their first two Series appearances ever, had the Yankees lost twice in a row. In between, they won 20 of the 25 Series in which they appeared.

World Series:
Most runs, career: 42, Mickey Mantle, New York (AL), 1951–53, 1960–64
Most extra base hits, career: 26, Mickey Mantle, New York (AL), 1951–53, 1955–58, 1960–64
Most total bases, career: 123, Mickey Mantle, New York (AL), 1951–53, 1955–58, 1960–64
Most home runs, career: 18, Mickey Mantle, New York (AL), 1951–53, 1955–58, 1960–64
Most runs batted in, career: 40, Mickey Mantle, New York (AL), 1951–53, 1955–58, 1960–64
Most walks, career; 43, Mickey Mantle, New York (AL), 1951–53, 1955–58, 1960–64
Most strikeouts, career: 54, Mickey Mantle, New York (AL), 1951–53, 1955–58, 1960–64

World Series, pitcher:
Most series: 11, Edward C. "Whitey" Ford, New York (AL), 1950, 1953, 1955–58, 1960–64
Most games, career: 22, E.C. "Whitey" Ford, New York (AL), 1950, 1953, 1955–58, 1960–64
Most games started, career: 22, E.C. "Whitey" Ford, New York (AL), 1950, 1953, 1955–58, 1960–64

Mickey Mantle connects for a first-pitch homer in the ninth inning off Barney Schultz to give the Yanks a 2–1 victory over the Cardinals in the 1964 World Series. *UPI*

Most games won, career: 10, E.C. "Whitey" Ford, New York (AL), 1950, 1953, 1955–58, 1960–64

Most games lost, career: 8, E.C. "Whitey" Ford, New York (AL), 1950, 1953, 1955–58, 1960–64

Most innings pitched, career: 146, E.C. "Whitey" Ford, New York (AL), 1950, 1953, 1955–58, 1960–64

Most runs allowed, career: 51, E.C. "Whitey" Ford, New York (AL), 1950, 1953, 1955–58, 1960–64

Most earned runs allowed, career: 44, E.C. "Whitey" Ford, New York (AL), 1950, 1953, 1955–58, 1960–64

Most hits allowed, career: 132, E.C. "Whitey" Ford, New York (AL), 1950, 1953, 1955–58, 1960–64

Most bases on balls, career: 34, E.C. "Whitey" Ford, New York (AL), 1950, 1953, 1955–58, 1960–64

Most strikeouts, career: 94, E.C. "Whitey" Ford, New York (AL), 1950, 1953, 1955–58, 1960–64

The Yankees' Whitey Ford owns many World Series marks.   *UPI*

Hitting the Wind

LOS ANGELES, Cal., Sept. 9, 1965—A pair of lefthanders locked horns in a pitching duel today and the result was very nearly a double no-hitter. Pitching for the hometown Dodgers was Sandy Koufax, with a flashy 21–7 record and the league lead in strikeouts with 318. Going for the Chicago Cubs was well-traveled Bob Hendley, sporting a 2–2 record.

Batters were helpless against the portsiders, failing to reach base for four innings. Then, in the bottom of the fifth, the Dodgers' Lou Johnson worked Hendley for a walk, to become the first base runner of the game. Ron Fairly sacrificed. Then Johnson stole third and, when catcher Chris Krug pegged the ball into leftfield, went on to score. Hendley lost the perfect

49

The Dodgers' Sandy Koufax threw four no-hitters. *Malcolm Emmons*

game, the shutout, and the lead, but still had his no-hitter intact. Koufax, meanwhile, was crafting a perfect game.

The pressure was mounting and in the seventh inning, it was Johnson, again, who figured in the play. With two out, he blooped a double down the leftfield line. He was left stranded, the only man to be left on base during the entire game.

Koufax proceeded to strike out Ron Santo, Ernie Banks, and rookie Byron Browne in the eighth. He ended the game by whiffing Krug and pinch-hitters Joey Amalfitano and Harvey Kuenn.

The no-hitter, marked by his 14 strikeouts, was the fourth for Koufax, one more than the number pitched by Cy Young, Bob Feller, and Larry Corcoran.

The total of just one hit in a game is a record.

Fewest hits, both teams, one game: 1, Chicago (0) and Los Angeles (1), National League, Sept. 9, 1965

MOE-ing Them Down

LOS ANGELES, Cal., Oct. 5, 1966—Moe Drabowsky, who shares the American League record of hitting four batters in one game, pitched his way into the record books again today. Hurling for the Baltimore Orioles against the Los Angeles Dodgers in the World Series opener, Drabowsky came on in relief of Dave McNally in the third inning.

He struck out Wes Parker, forced in a run by walking Jim Gilliam, and then retired John Roseboro to quell a Dodger uprising. Drabowsky fanned a record 11 batters in all, allowed only one hit, and protected the Orioles' lead as Baltimore went on to win, 5–2.

Cast off earlier this season by Kansas City, Drabowsky started the fourth inning today by striking out pinch-hitter Jim Barbieri. Maury Wills and Willie Davis were also retired via the strikeout route. The 31-year-old Drabowsky, born in Ozanna, Poland, then proceeded to fan three more Dodgers in the fifth—Lou Johnson, Tommy Davis, and Jim Lefebvre—to tie the record of six straight set by Cincinnati's Hod Eller against the White Sox in the scandal-tainted series of 1919. The 11 strikeouts by Drabowsky, a record total for a relief pitcher, bettered the mark of 10 by Jess Barnes of the Giants against the Yankees in 1921.

Drabowsky's four hit batsmen came in a regular-season game when he was pitching for the Chicago White Sox, June 2, 1957.

Frank Robinson (left), Moe Drabowsky (center), and Brooks Robinson enjoy the Orioles' 5–2 victory over the Dodgers in the 1966 World Series opener.   *UPI*

World Series:
Most strikeouts by a relief pitcher: 11, Myron W. "Moe" Drabowsky,
  Baltimore (AL), Oct. 5, 1966

A Long Time Coming

HOUSTON, Tex., April 16, 1968—How long can a team go without scoring a run in one game? It took Houston 24 innings starting last night before the Astros scored a run early this morning for a 1–0 victory over the New York Mets, ending the longest one-run shutout in baseball history.

Wade Blasingame, the fifth Astros' pitcher, was the winner in a game that saw each team collect 11 hits as the Mets used eight pitchers, starting with Tom Seaver.

Here's how the winning run was scored: Norm Miller walked in the bottom of the 24th inning and advanced to second base on a balk by Met pitcher Les Rohr. Jim Wynn was walked

The Mets' starting pitcher in the longest one-run shutout was Tom Seaver, who gave up two hits to the Astros before being relieved in the 10th inning.   *UPI*

intentionally. Then Rusty Staub moved the runners to second and third on an infield out. Another intentional walk, to Hal King, loaded the bases. Houston's Bob Aspromonte then hit what looked like a double play ball, but Met shortstop Al Weis turned it into a run-scoring bobble.

Longest 1–0 game: 24 innings, New York Mets vs. Houston (NL), April 15–16, 1968

Most innings caught, game: 24, Hal King, Houston (NL) and Jerry Grote, New York Mets (NL), April 15, 1968

53

Dandy Don

HOUSTON, Tex., July 9, 1968—Willie Mays of the San Francisco Giants scored an unearned run in the first inning, but it was enough to provide the National League with a 1–0 victory and give Don Drysdale his second straight All-Star Game decision.

Starting for the fifth time in eight All-Star Games, Drysdale extended this record appearance to 19⅓ innings and although he failed to fan anyone today, retained his career record of 19 strikeouts in All-Star competition.

Before the Los Angeles Dodger star displayed his mound mastery in the Astrodome, Drysdale learned that one of his regular-season records had been revised. Earlier this season he

The Dodgers' Don Drysdale pitched the most All-Star Game innings.

had pitched a record six straight shutouts and 58⅔ scoreless innings. Today, however, the Baseball Writers Association, custodian of baseball records, said it would consider only whole innings in the record. So Drysdale will be credited with only 58 shutout innings, two more than the former record of 56 pitched by Walter Johnson in 1913.

All-Star Game:
Most innings pitched: 19⅓, Don Drysdale, Los Angeles (NL), 1959–68
Most strikeouts: 19, Don Drysdale, Los Angeles (NL), 1959–68

All Over the Field

BLOOMINGTON, Minn., Sept. 22, 1968—Minnesota starting pitcher Cesar Tovar gave up no hits or runs, struck out one batter, walked one, and committed a balk in the first inning of tonight's game against the Oakland A's. Tovar, normally a shortstop, proceeded to play a different position each inning after that as the Twins beat Oakland, 2–1.

The first batter that Tovar faced on the mound was Bert Campaneris, who is the only other man to play all nine positions in a single major league game. He did it with the A's in Kansas City three seasons ago.

In addition to his pitching and errorless fielding, Tovar had one hit and scored a run in the Twins' triumph.

Most positions played, game: 9, Cesar Tovar, Minnesota (AL), vs. Oakland, September 22, 1968 (Ties Bert Campaneris,. Kansas City (AL), vs. California Angels, Sept. 8, 1965)

Gibby's ERA

ST. LOUIS, Mo., Sept. 26, 1968—St. Louis ace Bob Gibson hurled a six-hit shutout tonight en route to compiling the lowest earned-run average in major league history. The Cardinal righthander blanked the Houston Astros, 1–0, for his 13th shutout of the season and an ERA of 1.12. Gibson's mark betters the 51-year-old record of 1.22 set by Grover Cleveland Alexander in 1917.

Curt Flood drove in Mike Shannon in the home half of the fifth inning to provide Gibson with the only run he needed, as he struck out 11 Astros to raise his league-leading total to 268.

Bob Gibson of the Cardinals has the record for lowest earned-run average in a season. *UPI*

The victory was number 22, against 9 losses for Gibby as the World Series–bound Cardinals played before a crowd of 18,658.

Lowest earned-run average, season (minimum 300 innings pitched): 1.12, Bob Gibson, St. Louis (NL), 1968

Striking a Losing Pose

ST. LOUIS, Mo., Oct. 10, 1968—The Detroit Tigers captured the World Series by winning their third straight game today, 4–1, and not even strikeout king Bob Gibson could prevent it.

Gibson, who fanned a record 17 batters in the Series opener, struck out eight Tigers today in upping his World Series record total to 35. But in the end it was a game-winning rally that produced three runs in the seventh inning and gave Mickey Lolich his third victory of the Series and the Tigers the world championship.

World Series:
Most strikeouts, series: 35, Bob Gibson, St. Louis (NL), 1968
Most strikeouts, game: 17, Bob Gibson, St. Louis (NL), vs. Detroit, Oct. 2, 1968

Detroit's Mickey Lolich won three games in a single World Series against the Cardinals.   *UPI*

Most victories, series: 3, Mickey Lolich, Detroit Tigers (AL), 1968 (Ties Christy Mathewson, New York, (NL), 1905; Charles "Babe" Adams, Pittsburgh (NL), 1909; Jack Coombs, Philadelphia (AL), 1910; Urban Faber, Chicago (AL), 1917; Stan Coveleski, Cleveland (AL), 1920; Harry Brecheen, St. Louis (NL), 1946; Lew Burdette, Milwaukee (NL), 1957; Bob Gibson, St. Louis (NL), 1967)

Night All-Stars

CINCINNATI, Ohio, July 14, 1970—Despite a bipartisan start by President Richard Nixon, the first night All-Star Game ever played was an all-National League affair in Cincinnati's new Riverfront Stadium. Nixon, attending the game with daughter Julie and her husband, David Eisenhower, threw out two "first balls"—one to Cincinnati catcher Johnny Bench and one to AL starting receiver Bill Freehan of Detroit.

The Nationals scored three runs in the ninth inning and one in the 12th to defeat the Americans, 5–4, winning their eighth straight classic and their 12th in the last 13 games. The lone bright spot in the AL firmament was Boston's Carl Yastrzemski, who rapped three singles and a double in earning Most Valuable Player honors, the only thing the AL has won recently. The four hits by Yaz ties the number hit by Ducky Medwick of the Cardinals in the 1937 game and matched by Ted Williams of the Red Sox at Fenway Park in 1946.

The Red Sox' Ted Williams shares tips and an All-Star Game record with Carl Yastrzemski. *UPI*

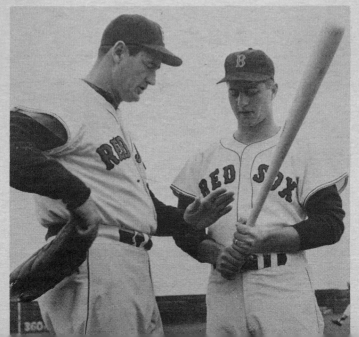

In bringing night All-Star baseball to the city where nighttime play was introduced to the big leagues, the Nationals won their sixth extra-inning game in six tries. The winning run scored on successive singles by the Reds' Pete Rose, Los Angeles's Billy Grabarkewitz, and Chicago's Jim Hickman.

All-Star Game:
Most hits, one game: 4, Carl Yastrzemski, Boston (AL), 1970 (Ties Joseph Medwick, St. Louis (NL), 1937; Ted Williams, Boston (AL), 1946)

Say Hey, One More Time

KANSAS CITY, Mo., July 24, 1973—It took a special ruling from Commissioner Bowie Kuhn to do it, but Willie Mays played in his 24th All-Star Game. Kuhn increased the player limit for the game so that stars such as Mays and California's no-hit pitcher Nolan Ryan could be included on the All-Star rosters. As a result, there were a record 58 players selected for the squads, 54 of whom saw action tonight in the National League's 7–1 victory in Royals Stadium, part of the new Harry S. Truman Sports Complex here.

Home runs by Cincinnati's Johnny Bench, San Francisco's Bobby Bonds, and Los Angeles's Willie Davis powered the NL to its 10th triumph in the last 11 games.

Mays, whose first 23 appearances were in a Giant uniform, was representing the New York Mets this year. And even though he was struck out by the Yankees' Sparky Lyle, who was in his first All-Star Game, Mays received a standing ovation from the crowd of 40,849.

All-Star Game:
Most at-bats: 75, Willie Mays, New York (NL), San Francisco (NL), New York (NL), 1951–73
Most runs: 20, Willie Mays, New York (NL), San Francisco (NL), New York (NL), 1951–73
Most hits: 23, Willie Mays, New York (NL), San Fransciso (NL), New York (NL), 1951–73
Most singles: 15, Willie Mays, New York (NL), San Francisco (NL), New York (NL), 1951–73
Most extra-base hits: 8, Willie Mays, New York (NL), San Francisco (NL), New York (NL), 1951–73
Most stolen bases: 6, Willie Mays, New York (NL), San Francisco (NL), New York (NL), 1951–73

Willie Mays played in 24 All-Star Games, setting numerous marks in the
process. *San Francisco Giants*

Record Relief

HOUSTON, Tex., Oct. 1, 1974—Relief pitcher Mike Marshall and his Los Angeles teammates prepared for the National League playoffs with an 8–5 victory tonight over the Houston Astros.

Marshall, who earlier this year had appeared in 13 consecutive games as a pitcher, was not particularly effective as he gave up two hits, walked six batters, and yielded four runs in the two innings he worked.

But the appearance did nothing to dim the overall season's performance of Marshall, who is pursuing a doctoral degree in kinesiology at Michigan State in the off-season. He has appeared in 106 games, shattering his own major league record of 92 set last season with the Montreal Expos. Marshall's 208 innings were also a season's record for a relief pitcher.

Most games, pitcher, season: 106, Mike Marshall, Los Angeles (NL), 1974
Most innings pitched, relief pitcher, season: 208, Mike Marshall, Los Angeles (NL), 1974

Hank Hammers No. 755

MILWAUKEE, Wis., July 20, 1976—Henry Aaron hit his 10th home run of the season and the 755th of his career tonight as he helped the Milwaukee Brewers defeat the California Angels, 6–2.

The 42-year-old Aaron, who came into the game batting just .247 as a part-time player, has had questions of retirement swirling around him since the season began. He has been playing in Milwaukee since the beginning of last season after being released by the Atlanta Braves, returning to the city in which he began his major league career in 1954 with the then Milwaukee Braves of the National League.

Of course, of all his home runs in a 23-year career, none was more memorable than the one he hit on April 8, 1978, in Fulton County Stadium as a member of the Atlanta Braves.

As he, and anyone else who was watching, recalls the scene, Los Angeles Dodgers' pitcher Al Downing went into a stretch, looked the runner back to first base, and fired home. The ball was straight and true, over the plate and rising slightly along the way. Aaron swung hard, unleashing power with a last instant snap of the wrists, and the ball sailed toward the leftfield fence.

Henry Aaron tells the media how he broke Babe Ruth's home run record.   *UPI*

Henry slowed to a trot rounding first base as he watched the ball elude the flailing reach of Bill Buckner, who had scaled the fence to lunge at it. The crowd was hammering, hooting, stomping, and whistling approval. Two teenage boys joined Aaron on his circuit of the bases. Dodger infielders congratulated him as he went by.

That was the 715th time Henry Aaron had hit a home run in a regular-season major league game, and it was the blast that moved Aaron to the top of the heap, ahead of Babe Ruth as the all-time leading hitter of home runs.

Today's 755th came off a pitcher named Mickey Scott in a game between two last-place teams.

Most home runs, career: 755, Henry Aaron, Milwaukee (NL), 1954–65; Atlanta (NL), 1966–74; Milwaukee (AL), 1975–76

As an Angel, Nolan Ryan passed the 300 mark in strikeouts in each of
five seasons.

Angel K

BALTIMORE, Md., Aug. 19, 1977—California Angel righthander Nolan Ryan became the first pitcher in major league
history to strike out 300 batters in five different seasons as he
fanned 11 Orioles in a 6–1 losing effort against Baltimore.

Third baseman Doug DeCinces was Ryan's sixth victim of
the evening and the 300th of the season as the fireballing native
of Refugio, Tex., was losing his 13th game against 17 victories.

The 30-year-old Ryan also owns the distinction of being the
only pitcher since 1900 to strike out 300 batters in three consecutive seasons. He turned the trick in 1972–74. He is also the
only pitcher in either league ever to strike out as many as 19
batters in a nine-inning game on two different occasions.

*Most seasons, 300 or more strikeouts: 5, Nolan Ryan, California (AL),
1972–74, 1976–77*

Mr. October

NEW YORK, Oct. 18, 1977—Reggie Jackson capped his first season as a New York Yankee by blasting three home runs to give the Bronx Bombers an 8–4 victory over the Los Angeles Dodgers as they won their first World Series in 15 years.

The flamboyant Jackson, who signed a multimillion-dollar free-agent contract with the Yankees after playing in Baltimore

Reggie Jackson powers his third home run as the Yankees win the game, 8–4, and the World Series against the Dodgers in 1977.   *UPI*

last season, was a controversial figure during the season, often feuding with manager Billy Martin and sometimes with his teammates in the dugout.

All that was forgotten tonight as he smacked the first pitch out of the park in three consecutive times at bat, driving in four runs. He also walked once and scored four times.

In his last nine times at bat in the six-game series, the 31-year-old Jackson hit five home runs, the last four in consecutive official times at bat.

World Series:
Most home runs, one series: 5, Reggie Jackson, New York (AL), 1977
Most runs, one series: 10, Reggie Jackson, New York (AL), 1977
Most home runs, game: 3, Reggie Jackson, New York (AL), Oct. 18, 1977 (Ties George H. "Babe" Ruth, New York (AL), Oct. 6, 1928)
Most total bases, game: 12, Reggie Jackson, New York (AL), Oct. 18, 1977 (Ties George H. "Babe" Ruth, New York (AL), Oct. 6, 1928)
Most home runs, consecutive times at bat: 4, Reggie Jackson, New York (AL), Oct. 16–18, 1977

King of Thieves

KANSAS CITY, Kan., Oct. 2, 1982—Rickey Henderson of the Oakland A's stole his 128th, 129th, and 130th bases of the season here today, and that's more than anyone has recorded since the 19th century when runners were credited with a stolen base for going from first to third on a single.

The stolen bases were in a losing cause as the A's lost to the Kansas City Royals, 5–4. But the victory didn't do much good for the second-place Royals either, since the California Angels won today and clinched the divisional pennant.

The 5-foot 10-inch, 180-pound Henderson, who was born on Christmas Day, 1958, in Chicago, had eclipsed Lou Brock's former modern record of 118 stolen bases more than a month ago, but injuries have reduced his playing time since then. All of his base running this season earned Henderson another major league record. He was caught stealing 42 times, an all-time high.

Most stolen bases, season (since 1900): 130, Rickey Henderson, Oakland (AL), 1982
Most times caught stealing, season: 42, Rickey Henderson, Oakland (AL), 1982

This was the steal by Rickey Henderson of the A's that broke Lou Brock's record of 118 stolen bases in 1982.   *UPI*

Gooden Plenty

NEW YORK, Nov. 13, 1985—Dwight Gooden, three days short of his 21st birthday, today became the youngest player ever to win the Cy Young Award, emblematic of the best pitcher in the league.

The New York Met righthander was a unanimous choice for his performance this year, his second in the major leagues, which included 24 victories against 4 losses and a 1.53 earned-run average in 276⅔ innings pitched. Gooden struck out 268 batters while walking 69 and allowing 51 runs, 47 of them earned.

The native of Tampa, Fla., started 35 games, completed 16, and hurled eight shutouts along the way.

Nicknamed "The Doctor" and sometimes called "Dr. K" for his strikeout proficiency, Gooden this past season led the major leagues in victories, ERA, and strikeouts, the first man to win the so-called pitching triple crown since Sandy Koufax turned the trick in 1966.

Youngest pitcher to win a Cy Young Award: Dwight Gooden, 20 years, 362 days old, New York (NL), 1985

When Dwight Gooden of the Mets captured the Cy Young Award in 1985, he was the youngest winner ever. *Mitchell Reibel*

20 Whiffs

BOSTON, Mass., April 29, 1986—Boston Red Sox righthander Roger Clemens, who underwent shoulder surgery eight months ago, today set a major league record by striking out 20 batters in a nine-inning game as the Bosox defeated the Seattle Mariners, 3–1.

The 20 strikeouts surpassed the previous record of 19 shared by Nolan Ryan of the California Angels in 1974, Tom Seaver of the New York Mets in 1970, and Steve Carlton of the St. Louis Cardinals in 1969. Only Tom Cheney of the Washington Senators has struck out more batters in a game, fanning 21 in 16 innings against Baltimore in 1962.

The Red Sox' Roger Clemens shows the game ball after his 20 strikeouts against the Mariners in 1986. *Wide World*

Along the way Clemens, who now has four victories and no defeats, struck out eight consecutive batters from the fourth to the sixth inning before Spike Owen flied to center. Clemens later struck out Owen in the ninth inning to tie the record before making Phil Bradley his 20th victim of the game.

Clemens, who had a 9–4 won-lost mark and 126 strikeouts in his rookie season two years ago, developed arm trouble last year. He had a 7–5 record pitching 98 innings with 74 strikeouts. On Aug. 30 he underwent surgery on his right shoulder and was out for the rest of the season.

Most strikeouts, nine-inning game: 20, Roger Clemens, Boston (AL), April 29, 1986
Most consecutive strikeouts, American League game: 8, Roger Clemens, Boston, April 29, 1986 (Ties Nolan Ryan, California, Aug. 7, 1973, and July 9, 1972)

Horner's Homers

ATLANTA, Ga., July 6, 1986—Atlanta Brave first baseman Bob Horner, who had never had more than two homers in a major league game, today became the 11th player in major league history to hit four home runs in a game.

The last player to hit four round-trippers in a game was Mike Schmidt of the Philadelphia Phillies, who turned the trick at Wrigley Field against the Chicago Cubs in a 10-inning contest on April 17, 1976. The last man to hit four homers in a nine-inning game was Willie Mays of the San Francisco Giants against the Milwaukee Braves on April 30, 1961.

The 28-year-old Horner is also the first man in this century—and the second in history—to hit four home runs in a losing cause, as the Montreal Expos beat the Braves, 11–8. Ed Delahanty, playing for the Phillies on July 13, 1896, hit four homers as Philadelphia lost to the Cubs, 9–8.

Horner led off the second inning with a solo shot and followed that with another bases-empty blast in the fourth. He then clouted a three-run homer in the fifth inning. After popping out in the seventh, Horner came to bat with two out in the bottom of the ninth. He whacked the first pitch off Montreal reliever Jeff Reardon over the left-centerfield fence. Horner's first three homers came off Expo starter Andy McGaffigan.

"In my wildest dreams I would never have expected to do

Atlanta's Bob Horner joined an elite group when he hit four home runs in one game aginst Montreal in 1986.   *Richard Pilling*

anything like that," Horner said after the game. "I had a good week today."

Most home runs, game: 4, Bob Horner, Atlanta (NL), July 6, 1986 (Ties Robert T. Lowe, Boston (NL), May 30, 1894; Edward Delahanty, Philadelphia (NL), July 13, 1896; Lou Gehrig, New York (AL), June 3, 1932; Chuck Klein, Philadelphia (NL), July 10, 1936; J. Patrick Seery, Chicago (AL), July 18, 1948; Gil Hodges, Brooklyn (NL), Aug. 31, 1950; Joseph Adcock, Milwaukee (NL), July 31, 1954; Rocky Colavito, Cleveland (AL), June 10, 1959; Willie Mays, San Francisco (NL), April 30, 1961; Mike Schmidt, Philadelphia (NL), April 17, 1976)

Fernando's Screwball

HOUSTON, Tex., July 15, 1986—With his screwball working to perfection, southpaw Fernando Valenzuela of the Los Angeles Dodgers struck out five straight batters in the All-Star Game tonight, matching the record established 52 years ago by Carl Hubbell of the New York Giants. The American League went on to win the game, however, 3–2.

Hubbell, also a lefthanded screwball artist, set down Babe

The Dodgers' Fernando Valenzuela tied an All-Star Game mark with his five consecutive strikeouts in 1986.   *Wide World*

Ruth, Lou Gehrig, Jimmie Foxx, Al Simmons, and Joe Cronin, all future Hall of Famers, in the 1934 All-Star Game.

Valenzuela's task was somewhat less formidable as he got Don Mattingly, Cal Ripken, and Jesse Barfield on swinging strikes in the fourth inning. He then caught Lou Whitaker looking in the fifth before getting fellow Mexican Teddy Higuera on a swinging strike. Higuera, the Milwaukee Brewer pitcher, had not batted in a regular-season game in six years because of the designated-hitter rule.

After recording the five consecutive Ks, the 26-year-old Valenzuela had his string snapped by Kirby Puckett, who bounced out to short.

All-Star Game:
Most consecutive strikeouts: 5, Fernando Valenzuela, Los Angeles (NL),
   July 15, 1986 (Ties Carl Hubbell, New York (NL), July 10, 1934)

Charlie Hustle

CINCINNATI, Ohio, Aug. 17, 1986—Cincinnati player-manager Pete Rose came in as a pinch-hitter today and looked at a third strike thrown by San Diego's Goose Gossage in a 9–5 Padres' triumph.

Depending on whether he decides to concentrate solely on managing from now on, it may have been the final plate appearance for the 45-year-old native of Cincinnati.

The 5-foot 11-inch, 200-pound Rose has been reluctantly winding down since he broke Ty Cobb's career record of 4,191 base hits in Cincinnati on Sept. 11, 1985, with a single off San Diego righthander Eric Show—57 years to the day that Cobb last came to bat.

In his last 10 at-bats, Rose hasn't had a hit, but just prior to that, on Aug. 14, he went 3-for-4 and drove in a run to lead the Reds to a 2–0 victory over the San Francisco Giants.

His career batting average is .303 and his many major league records are eloquent testimony to 24 years of achievement and hustle.

Most base hits, career: 4,256, Peter E. Rose, Cincinnati (NL), 1963–78;
   Philadelphia (NL), 1978–1983; Montreal (NL) and Cincinnati (NL),
   1984; Cincinnati (NL), 1985–86
Most plate appearances, career: 15,890, Peter E. Rose
Most times on base, career: 5,930, Peter E. Rose
Most games, career: 3,562, Peter E. Rose

The Reds' Pete Rose watches the hit that broke Ty Cobb's record in 1985. *Wide World*

Most seasons 150 or more games: 17, Peter E. Rose
Most seasons 100 or more games: 23, Peter E. Rose
Most at bats, career: 14,053, Peter E. Rose
Most seasons 600 or more at bats: 17, Peter E. Rose
Most consecutive seasons 600 or more at bats: 13, Peter E. Rose
Most runs scored, National League career: 2,165, Peter E. Rose
Most seasons leading major leagues in base hits: 7, Peter E. Rose (Ties
   Ty Cobb)
Most singles, career: 3,215, Peter E. Rose

PRO FOOTBALL

Nevers-Nevers Land

CHICAGO, Ill., Nov. 28, 1929—The holiday air permeated snow-covered Comiskey Park today as a Thanksgiving Day crowd of 8,000 watched the Bears and Cardinals battle for the championship of Chicago. Earlier, the two teams had played a scoreless tie, and with losing records neither was headed for a championship of anything but the Windy City.

An injured Red Grange said he was ready to play for the Bears, and an overweight, overage Jim Thorpe came out of retirement again to put in a token appearance with the Cardinals and add to the holiday festivities. Thorpe wasn't going to be much help to the South Siders, but the Cards were counting on powerful Ernie Nevers, the product of Superior, Wis., who went to Stanford and almost single-handedly took on Notre Dame's Four Horsemen in the 1925 Rose Bowl.

Nevers scored the second time the Cards had the ball, going 20 yards in the swirling snow behind a block by Duke Slater. Before the first half was over, Nevers scored twice more and booted a pair of extra points to give the Cardinals a 20–0 halftime lead.

The second half was almost a carbon copy of the first, with Nevers scoring three more touchdowns and kicking two points after. The Bears tallied on a 60-yard pass from Walt Homer to Garland Grange, Red's brother. Nevers's six touchdowns established an NFL record, as did his total of 40 points.

Most points scored, game: 40, Ernie Nevers, Chicago Cardinals, vs. Chicago Bears, Nov. 28, 1929 (6 touchdowns, 4 PATs)

Hutson's Haul

BOSTON, Mass., Nov. 18, 1945—The Alabama Antelope, Don Hutson, came off the bench today to catch five of the eight passes thrown his way, score a touchdown, gain six yards rushing, and kick four extra points in the Green Bay Packers' 28–0 triumph over the Boston Yanks before a crowd of more than 30,000 in Fenway Park.

The 6-foot 1-inch, 190-pound Hutson, who played in the 1935 Rose Bowl when Dixie Howell was the 'Bama quarterback, has been doing more place-kicking than pass-catching this season, his 11th as a pro. But Hutson was catching them today, and the

Green Bay's Don Hutson caught a record 99 touchdown passes.   *UPI*

10-yard scoring pitch from Irv Comp in the second quarter extended his record total of touchdown receptions to 99.

Hutson, who has led the NFL in scoring five times, is the only player ever to be honored twice as MVP—he was singled out in 1941 and again in 1942 as the NFL's top player.

Most touchdowns on pass receptions, career: 99, Don Hutson, Green Bay Packers, 1935–45

Jim Benton of the Cleveland Rams totaled 303 yards on pass receptions in one game in 1945.

Ram Catcher

DETROIT, Mich., Nov. 22, 1945—Don Hutson, move over, Jim Benton has arrived. The 6-foot 3-inch, 210-pound Benton was on the receiving end of 10 Bob Waterfield passes today as the Cleveland Rams sewed up the NFL's Western Division championship with a 28–21 decision over the Detroit Lions.

Benton, who scored two touchdowns and set up a third with his receptions, accounted for 303 yards, breaking the mark of 237 yards set by the Green Bay veteran, Don Hutson, two years ago. Waterfield completed only two other passes all day, for 26 yards, as more than 40,000 chilled Lion fans watched in Briggs Stadium.

Most yardage on pass receptions, game: 303 yards, Jim Benton, Cleveland Rams, vs. Detroit Lions, Nov. 22, 1945

The Los Angeles Rams' Norm Van Brocklin passed for 544 yards against the New Yankees in 1951. *UPI*

Groundless Fears

LOS ANGELES, Cal., Dec. 3, 1950—Led by the pass-catching of Tom Fears, the Los Angeles Rams went on a record-setting binge today in beating the Green Bay Packers, 51–14, to clinch at least a tie for the championship of the NFL's National Conference.

As the Rams were establishing seasonal records in 10 team offensive categories, the 6-foot 2-inch, 215-pound Fears was catching a record 18 passes to establish a single-game mark. The old league record of 14 receptions was set in 1940 by Don Looney of Philadelphia, and tied by Green Bay's Don Hutson in 1942, the Chicago Bears' Jimmy Keane in 1949, and the New York Bulldogs' Ralph Heywood in 1949.

With Norm Van Brocklin and Bob Waterfield passing, receivers like Fears and Elroy Hirsch, and runners like Glenn Davis and Tank Younger, the Rams have been an explosive offensive team all season. Just two weeks ago, against the New York Yanks, the Rams gained 636 yards, while the Yanks were picking up 497 yards to establish a record for most yards gained by two teams in one game: 1,133.

Most receptions, game: 18, Tom Fears, Los Angeles Rams, vs. Green Bay Packers, Dec. 3, 1950
Most yards gained, both teams, game: 1,133, Los Angeles Rams (636) and New York Yanks (497), Nov. 19, 1950

The Flingin' Dutchman

LOS ANGELES, Cal., Sept. 28, 1951—Young Norm Van Brocklin made Ram fans forget about the injured Bob Waterfield and Glenn Davis tonight as he passed for 554 yards in leading Los Angeles past the New York Yanks, 54–14.

Van Brocklin, who played college ball at Oregon, bettered the efforts of Chicago Bear quarterback Johnny Lujack, who passed for 468 yards two years ago.

Playing before a crowd of 30,315, Van Brocklin threw five touchdown aerials, four of them to Elroy "Crazylegs" Hirsch. The Rams' 34 first downs and 735 total yards also established league marks.

Most yardage, passing, game: 554, Norm Van Brocklin, Los Angeles Rams, vs. New York Yanks, Sept. 28, 1951
Most yards gained, game, one team: 735, Los Angeles Rams, vs. New York Yanks, Sept. 28, 1951

On the Right Track

LOS ANGELES, Cal., Dec 14, 1952—Dick "Night Train" Lane put the Los Angeles Rams into a playoff with the Detroit Lions, but he won't be there to enjoy the fruits of his labor.

Lane intercepted three passes and ran back one for a touchdown today to spark the defending champion Rams to their eighth straight victory, a 28–14 decision over Pittsburgh. The three interceptions gave Lane a record total of 14 for the season, surpassing the mark of 12 shared by Don Sandifer of Washington and Spec Sanders of the old New York Yankees.

A crowd of more than 70,000 was on hand to see Norm Van Brocklin throw a touchdown pass to Elroy Hirsch and two to Tom Fears as Bob Waterfield, in his last game for the Rams, was relegated to kicking extra points.

Pittsburgh quarterback Jim Finks was victimized four times by the Ram defense, and it was the last interception that brought Lane the record and put him out of the playoff game. Lane, a product of Scottsbluff (Neb.) Junior College, was brought down hard after the interception, wrenching his knee and severely spraining his ankle.

Most interceptions, season: 14, Dick "Night Train" Lane, Los Angeles Rams, 1952

Dick "Night Train" Lane of the Detroit Lions holds the NFL record with 14 interceptions in a season. *UPI*

Green Bay's Paul Hornung scores against Los Angeles in the final game
of his 176-point season.   *UPI*

Golden Boy

LOS ANGELES, Cal., Dec. 17, 1960—Paul Hornung scored a
fourth-quarter touchdown and followed that with his fifth extra
point of the day to lead the Green Bay Packers past the Los
Angeles Rams, 35–21, and on to their first divisional championship in 16 years.

Hornung, called "the Golden Boy" because of his golden
locks and ability to come up with the "money play," scored on
a one-yard plunge. The score, and extra points, brought his
season's point total to a record 176. Hornung, who won the
Heisman Trophy four years ago as a quarterback at Notre Dame,
had broken the old scoring record of 138 points two weeks ago
when he scored 23 points against the Chicago Bears. The record that Hornung broke had been set by Don Hutson in 1942.
Hutson, incidentally, was on that last Packer team to win a
divisional title, in 1944.

*Most points, season: 176, Paul Hornung, Green Bay Packers, 1960 (15
touchdowns, 41 PATs, 15 field goals)*

Running Wild

CHICAGO, Ill., Dec. 12, 1965—With the NFL's Western Division championship at stake, Chicago's Gale Sayers went on a scoring binge today in tying a 36-year-old record with a six-touchdown performance against the San Franciso 49ers. Winning today, 61–20, kept the Bears in contention with the Baltimore Colts and Green Bay Packers. (In Baltimore, Green Bay's Paul Hornung scored five TDs in a 42–27 Packer triumph.)

The 6-foot, 200-pound Sayers, a rookie out of Kansas University, opened the scoring after gathering in a screen pass from Rudy Bukich. The play covered 80 yards, all of it on Sayers's running. The soft-spoken halfback then scored on runs of 21, 7, 50, and 1 yard before returning a punt 85 yards for his sixth touchdown, matching the number scored by Ernie Nevers of the Chicago Cardinals against the Bears on Thanksgiving Day, 1929, and Dub Jones of Cleveland, also against the Bears, in 1951.

After the game, Sayers was awarded the game ball and thus became the first player in Bear history to be awarded two game balls in one season. In addition to his TDs, Sayers picked up 113 yards rushing, 89 yards on pass receptions, and 134 yards on punt returns.

On no count was it a great day for the 49ers, especially for

Gale Sayers of the Chicago Bears heads toward one of his six touchdowns in a game against the San Francisco 49ers in 1965.   *UPI*

placekicker Tommy Davis. He missed an extra-point attempt. It was the first extra point he failed to convert since he began playing in the NFL in 1959. The onetime Louisiana State star had kicked a record 234 points in a row.

Most touchdowns, game: 6, Gale Sayers, Chicago Bears, vs. San Francisco 49ers, Dec. 12, 1965 (Ties Ernie Nevers, Chicago Cardinals, vs. Chicago Bears, Nov. 28, 1929; William "Dub" Jones, Cleveland Browns, vs. Chicago Bears, Nov. 25, 1951)
Most consecutive extra points: 234, Tommy Davis, San Francisco 49ers, Sept. 27, 1959, to Dec. 5, 1965

Doing It Up Brown

ST. LOUIS, Mo., Dec. 21, 1965—The Cleveland Browns' Jim Brown, as stormy in temperament as he is talented in football, saw most of his last regular-season game from the bench today. Big No. 32 was ejected from the game in the first half after fighting with the St. Louis Cardinals' Joe Robb.

Before he left the game, though, the 6-foot 3-inch, 230-pound Brown gained 74 yards on 11 carries, scored his 21st touchdown of the season, the 127th of his career. His touchdown contributed to Cleveland's 27–24 victory over St. Louis that gave the Browns the best record in the NFL with 11 wins and 3 losses.

Earlier in the season, Brown became the first player to rush for 100 touchdowns in a career. Among the records of Brown, who never missed a game in his nine-year career, are:

Most touchdowns, career: 126, Jim Brown, Cleveland Browns, 1957–65
Most seasons leading the league, touchdowns: 5, Jim Brown, Cleveland Browns, 1957–59, 1963, 1965
Highest rushing average, career: 5.22 yards per carry, Jim Brown, Cleveland Browns, 1957–65
Most seasons leading the league, rushing: 8, Jim Brown, Cleveland Browns, 1957–61, 1963–65

Just for Kicks

PITTSBURGH, Pa., Sept. 24, 1967—Jim Bakken has nothing to kick about now. The former reserve quarterback from the University of Wisconsin and full-time kicking specialist for the St. Louis Cardinals booted a record seven field goals today as St. Louis beat Pittsburgh, 28–14.

Cleveland's Jim Brown scores the last touchdown of his career, against the St. Louis Cardinals.   *UPI*

In addition to making kicks of 18, 24, 33, 29, 24, 32, and 23 yards today, Bakken missed two attempts, from 45 and 50 yards away. The nine attempts are also an NFL record.

Bakken's harvest surpassed the six field goals registered last season by Garo Yepremian of the Detroit Lions against the Minnesota Vikings.

The contribution of the Cardinals' Larry Wilson went largely unnoticed. "Don't I get any credit for holding the ball?" Wilson asked after the game.

Most field goals attempted, game: 9, Jim Bakken, St. Louis Cardinals, vs. Pittsburgh Steelers, Sept. 24, 1967

Most field goals, game: 7, Jim Bakken, St. Louis Cardinals, vs. Pittsburgh Steelers, Sept. 24, 1967

Kapp-ital Performance

BLOOMINGTON, Minn., Sept. 28, 1969—Most sports fans' minds were on baseball today as the Atlanta Braves clinched the National League's Western Division pennant to join the New York Mets, Minnesota Twins, and Baltimore Orioles in baseball's new-fangled intra-league playoffs that were instituted this season.

But Chicano Joe Kapp and the Minnesota Vikings put on a record-breaking performance that made folks in Metropolitan Stadium here forget about the summer sport. Kapp, the University of California quarterback who played in Canada before becoming a Viking, hit six different receivers with seven touchdown passes, equaling the passing performances of Sid Luckman in 1943, Y. A. Tittle in 1962, George Blanda in 1961, and Adrian Burk in 1954. Burk, who played for the Philadelphia Eagles, was on the field today, working the game as a back judge.

With Vice President Spiro Agnew—former governor of Maryland—in the stands to root for the defending champion Baltimore Colts, Kapp hit Gene Washington twice and Dave Osborn, Bob Grim, Kent Kramer, John Beasley, and Jim Lindsey once each to lead Minnesota past Baltimore, 52–14. Overall, Kapp connected with 12 different receivers in passing for 499 yards before a sellout crowd of 47,644.

Most touchdown passes thrown, game: 7, Joe Kapp, Minnesota Vikings, vs. Baltimore Colts, Sept. 28, 1969 (Ties Sid Luckman, Chicago Bears, vs. New York Giants, Nov. 14, 1943; Adrian Burk, Philadelphia Eagles, vs. Washington Redskins, Oct. 17, 1954; George Blanda, Houston Oilers, vs. New York Titans, Nov. 19, 1961; Y. A. Tittle, New York Giants, vs. Washington Redskins, Oct. 28, 1962)

Mighty Foot

NEW ORLEANS, La., Nov. 8, 1970—Trailing 17–16 with two seconds left to play and the ball on their own 45-yard line, New

Minnesota's Joe Kapp passed for seven touchdowns against Baltimore in 1969.

Malcolm Emmons

This is the special shoe Tom Dempsey of the New Orleans Saints wore for his record field goal against the Detroit Lions in 1970.   *UPI*

Orleans Saints' coach, J.D. Roberts sent in kicking specialist Tom Dempsey to try a field goal against the Detroit Lions. The 6-foot 1-inch, 265-pound Dempsey set up 10 yards behind the line of scrimmage, with holder Joe Scarpati kneeling at the Lion 37. Jackie Burkett snapped the ball, Scarpati set it down, and Dempsey kicked.

The final gun sounded just before the cheers erupted from the 66,910 fans in Tulane's Sugar Bowl Stadium as the ball sailed through the uprights. The 63-yard kick was the longest field goal ever made in an NFL game, surpassing the old record of 56 yards by Baltimore's Bert Rechichar against the Chicago Bears in 1953.

Dempsey, who was born without a right hand and with a clubbed right foot, the one he kicks with, said afterward he couldn't even see the goal posts. But he didn't have to see that far. "I saw the referee's hands go up and everybody started yelling and I knew it was good," Dempsey recounted happily.

Longest field goal: 63 yards, Tom Dempsey, New Orleans Saints, vs. Detroit Lions, Nov. 8, 1970

Starr Billing

MIAMI, Fla., Dec. 19, 1971—The last time Bart Starr had walked off the field in the Orange Bowl the grass was real and the glory was his. That was nearly four years ago, after Green Bay had won its second straight Super Bowl.

Today, the 37-year-old Starr was a loser, beaten by Miami on artificial grass, 27–6, in the final game of the season, the last of his 16-year career. The former Alabama quarterback—known as a "coach on the field" in the Super Bowl years—underwent arm surgery before this season and had been used sparingly. But coach Dan Devine went with him all the way today.

In the final days of his career, Green Bay's Bart Starr maneuvers, looking for a receiver. *San Diego Chargers*

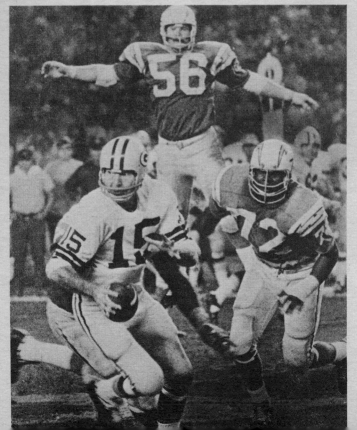

Starr was his usual proficient self, completing 13 of 22 passes for 126 yards, but he couldn't avert a last-place finish in the NFC's Central Division with a record of four wins, eight losses, and two ties.

But Starr could look back on many notable achievements, one in particular that attested to his accuracy. In 1964–65 he threw 294 consecutive passes without being intercepted, an NFL record.

Most consecutive passes with no interceptions: 294, Bart Starr, Green Bay Packers, 1964–65

Jack Be Nimble, Jack Be Quick

GREEN BAY, Wis., Sept. 24, 1972—The oldest record in the books was erased today by quick and alert Jack Tatum and a misjudgment by the officials.

Tatum, playing safety for the Oakland Raiders, scooped up a bouncing football in one end zone and raced 104 yards down the sideline to the other end of the field for a touchdown that provided the margin of victory in Oakland's 20–14 victory over the Green Bay Packers. The officials ruled that the loose ball had been fumbled by MacArthur Lane and could legally be advanced. Videotape replay later showed, however, that Lane had bobbled a pitchout and never had control of the ball. In that case, Tatum should not have been able to advance it.

But it was ruled a fumble, and so Tatum's name replaces that of George Halas of the Chicago Bears, who picked up a fumble and traveled 98 yards with it against the Oorang Indians in an NFL game Nov. 4, 1923.

Longest return of a recovered opponent's fumble: 104 yards, Jack Tatum, Oakland Raiders, vs. Green Bay Packers, Sept. 24, 1972

Return of the Cowboy

ST. LOUIS, Mo., Oct. 13, 1974—Dallas rookie Dennis Morgan opened the scoring today with a record-tying punt return, but it wasn't enough to bring victory to the Cowboys. The St. Louis Cardinals won their fifth straight game of the season, 31–28.

The 5-foot 11-inch, 200-pound Morgan, a 10th-round draft choice out of Western Illinois, gathered in a Hal Roberts punt on his own 2-yard line and weaved his way through the defense 98 yards for a touchdown.

The jaunt tied the NFL record for longest return of a punt, shared by Gil LeFevre of the old Cincinnati Reds and Charlie West of the Minnesota Vikings.

Longest punt return: 98 yards, Dennis Morgan, Dallas Cowboys, vs. St. Louis Cardinals, Oct. 13, 1974 (Ties Charlie West, Minnesota Vikings, vs. Washington Redskins, Nov. 3, 1968, and Gil LeFevre, Cincinnati Reds, vs. Brooklyn Dodgers, Dec. 3, 1933)

The Scrambler's Legacy

LOS ANGELES, Cal., Dec. 31, 1978—Quarterback Fran Tarkenton had made it to three Super Bowls with the Minnesota Vikings, but the Los Angeles Rams derailed the Vikings today, 34–10, in the NFC divisional playoffs.

It was Tarkenton's last game in a celebrated 18-year career that began in 1961 with the infant Vikings, when he was a third-round draft choice out of Georgia. Traded to the New York Giants in 1967, he came back to the Vikings in 1972, and now it's all over.

Fran Tarkenton left his marks in the book.   *UPI*

"The Scrambler," as he was known, went out on top even if he never won a Super Bowl. He started his first game and he started his last one. He played in more games than any other quarterback in the history of pro football (257). He posted career records for most passes completed (3,686) and most passes attempted (6,467), most yards gained passing (47,003), and most touchdown passes (342).

Most passes completed, career: 3,686, Fran Tarkenton, Minnesota Vikings, 1961–66, 1972–78; New York Giants, 1967–71
Most passes attempted, career: 6,467, Fran Tarkenton, Minnesota Vikings, 1961–66, 1972–76; New York Giants, 1967–71
Most yards gained passing, career: 47,003, Fran Tarkenton, Minnesota Vikings, 1961–66, 1972–76; New York Giants, 1967–71
Most touchdown passes, career: 342, Fran Tarkenton, Minnesota Vikings, 1961–66, 1972–76; New York Giants, 1967–71
Most games at quarterback, career: 257, Fran Tarkenton, Minnesota Vikings, 1961–66, 1972–76; New York Giants, 1967–71

Ageless Viking

FOXBORO, Mass., Dec. 16, 1979—For 41-year-old Jim Marshall it was farewell today. The 6-foot 4-inch, 240-pound defensive end of the Minnesota Vikings played the final game of a 20-year career.

It was tarnished only slightly by the fact that the New England Patriots beat the Vikings, 27–23, but Marshall's lifetime marks will be remembered more than the score of the game.

A Kentuckian who played for Ohio State before breaking in with the Cleveland Browns in 1960, Marshall joined the Vikings in their first year in 1961 and played in every game since then.

His 282 consecutive games are an NFL record. So are his 19 seasons with one club and his 29 opponents' fumbles recovered.

Most consecutive games played, career: 282, Jim Marshall, Cleveland Browns, 1960; Minnesota Vikings, 1961–79
Most seasons, one club: 19, Jim Marshall, Minnesota Vikings, 1961–79
Most opponents' fumbles recovered: 29, Jim Marshall, Cleveland Browns 1960; Minnesota Vikings, 1961–79

The Cardinals' Roy Green sped 106 yards on a kickoff return in 1979.

St. Louis Cardinals

A Touch of Green

IRVING, Tex., Oct. 21, 1979—Roy Green of the St. Louis Cardinals, a rookie safety out of Henderson State, was six yards in his own end zone today when he took a Dallas kickoff.

He was touched only once—by an off-balance arm swipe by Doug Cosbie on the Cardinal 40—as he sped to a touchdown and into the record book. His 106-yard romp tied the mark shared by Al Carmichael of the Green Bay Packers and Noland Smith of the Kansas City Chiefs.

It was the Cardinals' only touchdown as Dallas prevailed, 22–13. Green said, "I guess someday the record will be broken . . . maybe by me."

Longest return of a kickoff: 106 yards, Roy Green, St. Louis Cardinals, vs. Dallas Cowboys, Oct. 21, 1979 (Ties Noland Smith, Kansas City Chiefs, vs. Denver Broncos, Dec. 17, 1967; Al Carmichael, Green Bay Packers, vs. Chicago Bears, Oct. 7, 1956)

Have Gun, Will Shoot!

NEW YORK, Sept. 21, 1980—If there was any solace for the New York Jets today, it came from the pitching performance of Richard Todd. While the San Francisco 49ers were handing the winless Jets their third straight setback, 37–27, Todd completed a record 42 passes.

The Jet quarterback, who threw three touchdown passes in a catch-up game, broke the 16-year-old single-game completion record of 37, set by George Blanda with Houston in the AFL.

Todd's 59 attempts didn't approach Blanda's record 68.

Most passes completed, game: 42, Richard Todd, New York Jets, vs. San Francisco 49ers, Sept. 21, 1980

Return of the Century

SAN DIEGO, Cal., Nov. 8, 1981—It was not one of Dan Fouts's best days. The San Diego Charger quarterback fumbled once, was sacked six times, and threw two interceptions as the Cincinnati Bengals routed the Chargers, 40–17.

On the other hand, for Bengal cornerback Louis Breeden it was a glorious day. With 36 seconds remaining in the first half and the Bengals holding a 24–7 lead, the Chargers were on the Cincinnati four-yard line. Fouts lofted a pass intended for Charlie Joiner, but Breeden grabbed it in the end zone and took off. A few good blocks helped, and the four-year veteran out of North Carolina Central sped the distance—102 yards for a touchdown.

It tied the NFL record for longest return of an intercepted pass.

Longest return of an intercepted pass: 102 yards, Louis Breeden, Cincinnati Bengals, vs. San Diego Chargers, Nov. 8, 1981 (Ties Gary Barbero, Kansas City Chiefs, vs. Seattle Seahawks, Dec. 11, 1977; Erich Barnes, New York Giants, vs. Dallas Cowboys, Oct. 22, 1961; and Bob Smith, Detroit Lions, vs. Chicago Bears, Nov. 24, 1949)

Five for the Road

OAKLAND, Cal., Nov. 22, 1981—For six weeks, tight end Kellen Winslow of the San Diego Chargers hadn't caught a touchdown pass, and he was beginning to wonder if he'd ever catch another one.

No need for him to worry. The 6-foot 6-inch, 250-pound Winslow erased all fears when he caught an NFL record-tying five touchdown passes today in a 55-21 swamping of the Oakland Raiders.

Dan Fouts, flight director of Air Coryell, threw the first four of the TD passes; Chuck Muncie tossed the fifth before a stunned Raiders' crowd at the Coliseum.

The Chargers' Kellen Winslow caught a record five touchdown passes in a game against the Raiders in 1981. *San Diego Chargers*

"My number was called a lot and I was just able to come through," Winslow shrugged modestly. "I just happened to be in the right place at the right time."

By himself, Winslow got 30 points with receptions of 15, 29, 4, 5, and 3 yards.

Winslow tied the 1950 mark of Bob Shaw of the Chicago Cardinals.

Most touchdowns on pass receptions, game: 5, Kellen Winslow, San Diego Chargers, vs. Oakland Raiders, Nov. 22, 1981 (Ties Bob Shaw, Chicago Cardinals, vs. Baltimore Colts, Oct. 2, 1950)

Bull's-Eye

HOUSTON, Tex., Jan. 2, 1983—Ken Anderson, "Mr. Accuracy," threaded the needle with the precision of a seamstress today when he threw a record 20 consecutive completions as the Cincinnati Bengals defeated the Houston Oilers, 35–27.

Winding up the regular season as the NFL's top-rated passer for the second year in a row, the Bengals' quarterback had a completion percentage for the year of 70.55 (218 of 309), which broke Sammy Baugh's NFL record of 70.33, set with the Washington Redskins in 1945.

As added testimony to his accuracy, Anderson was the only NFL quarterback to throw more than 300 passes and keep his interceptions under 10. He had just nine in the course of guiding the Bengals into the playoffs.

Anderson, a product of little Augustana College in Rock Island, Ill., also holds the record for highest pass-completion percentage in a game, 90.91 percent.

Most consecutive passes completed: 20, Ken Anderson, Cincinnati Bengals, vs. Washington Redskins, Jan. 2, 1983
Highest completion percentage, season: 70.55 percent, Ken Anderson, Cincinnati Bengals, 1982 (218 of 309)

Dorsett's Dash

MINNEAPOLIS, Minn., Jan. 3, 1983—The Minnesota Vikings were leading the Dallas Cowboys, 24–13, in the final quarter tonight, and Dallas was on its own one-yard line following Timmy Newsome's fumble of a kickoff.

Cincinnati's Ken Anderson connected for 20 in a row in 1983.

Ira Golden

A noisy home crowd of 60,000 in the Metrodome suddenly came to its feet when Tony Dorsett burst up the middle on first down, broke to the outside, and shot up the right sideline. At the 30, he brushed off a tackle by Willie Teal and went on to an NFL-record 99-yard run.

Dorsett's gallop was to no avail, however, as the Vikings wound up winning the game, 31–27.

The longest run from scrimmage had been 97 yards by Bob Gage of the Pittsburgh Steelers against the Chicago Bears on Dec. 4, 1949, and Andy Uram of the Green Bay Packers against the Chicago Cardinals on Oct. 8, 1939.

Longest run from scrimmage: 99 yards, Tony Dorsett, Dallas Cowboys, vs. Minnesota Vikings, Jan. 3, 1983 (TD)

Dallas's Tony Dorsett got off a 99-yard run against Minnesota in 1983.
Dallas Cowboys

Ali and "The Diesel"

WASHINGTON, D.C., December 17, 1983—John Riggins, the Washington Redskins' fullback, ran 44 yards today for an NFL-record 24th touchdown of the season as the Redskins defeated the New York Giants, 31–22, and won the NFC Eastern Division championship.

It was a comeback victory for favored Washington, which was behind, 12–7, at the half due to the gifted foot of Giant rookie Ali Haji-Sheikh, who kicked four field goals before intermission. Haji-Sheikh added a fifth three-pointer in the second half to give him 35 for season, breaking the NFL mark set by the New York Jets' Jim Turner in 1968.

Earlier in the year, Riggins, called the "The Diesel," had broken the 19-TD rushing record of Jimmy Taylor of the Green Bay Packers, set in 1962.

Washington also wound up with the league mark for points scored in a season (541, erasing the Houston Oilers' total of 513 in 1961).

Most touchdowns rushing, season: 24, John Riggins, Washington Redskins, 1983
Most field goals, season: 35, Ali Haji-Sheikh, New York Giants, 1983
Most points, season: 541, Washington Redskins, 1983

Washington's John Riggins scored the most touchdowns ever in a season.

UPI

Nobody has ever gained as many yards rushing in a season as the Los
Angeles Rams' Eric Dickerson. *Vic Milton*

Unbelievable Eric

SAN FRANCISCO, Cal., Dec. 14, 1984—Eric Dickerson, the
Los Angeles Rams' sensational second-year running back, ran
into a wall of San Francisco 49er defenders tonight. Poor Eric;
he gained only 98 yards as the 15–1 49ers held off the 10–6
Rams, 19–16, in their final regular-season game.

For the 23-year-old Dickerson, it was still one whale of a
season. A week ago, against Houston, he'd rushed for 215
yards to vault past O. J. Simpson's 11-year-old mark of 2,003
yards gained rushing in a season. He ended the year with 2,105
yards and this comment from coach John Robinson: "When-

ever Eric doesn't do something unbelievable, you're disappointed. He's just, uh, *pretty good.*"

Most yards gained rushing, season: 2,105, Eric Dickerson, Los Angeles Rams, 1984

Magnetic Monk

WASHINGTON, D.C., Dec. 16, 1984—"Art Monk could catch a BB in the dark if he heard the gun go off," said Washington Redskins' receivers coach Charley Taylor.

Taylor's description followed Monk's performance today when he caught 11 passes for a season-record 106 as the Redskins edged St. Louis, 29–27.

With Monk scoring two touchdowns, capping a spectacular year, Washington won its third consecutive NFC East championship.

The Redskins' No. 1 draft pick in 1980, out of Syracuse, Monk broke the record of 101, set by Charlie Hennigan of the Houston Oilers in 1964.

Most passes caught, season: 106, Art Monk, Washington Redskins, 1984

Splash of the Dolphins

MIAMI, Fla., Dec. 17, 1984—A winning combination all season long, Miami Dolphin quarterback Dan Marino and wide receiver Mark Clayton clicked tonight for a touchdown in the final minute of play to knock the Dallas Cowboys out of the NFL playoffs, 28–21.

It was Clayton's third touchdown reception of the game, giving him 18 for the season, an NFL mark, and it also enabled Marino to finish the year with 48 touchdown passes, 362 completions, and 5,084 yards passing.

Clayton's 18 erased the old mark of 17 jointly held by Don Hutson of the Green Bay Packers, Elroy Hirsch of the Los Angeles Rams, and Bill Groman of the Houston Oilers.

Earlier in the season Marino had surpassed the record 36 touchdown passes held by Houston's George Blanda and Y. A. Tittle of the New York Giants.

Miami's Dan Marino threw the most touchdown passes in a season in 1984.
Miami Dolphins

Most touchdown receptions, season: 18, Mark Clayton, Miami Dol-
  phins, 1984
Most touchdown passes, season: 48, Dan Marino, Miami Dolphins,
  1984

103

Quick Ending

PHILADELPHIA, Pa., Nov. 10, 1985—Rick Donnelly's 62-yard punt for Atlanta had pinned Philadelphia on its one-yard line. The score was 17–17 today and the game was in overtime. The Eagles were perilously close to being the first team to lose an overtime game on a safety.

So Eagle quarterback Ron Jaworski passed to wide receiver Mike Quick at the 20, and he turned the short pass into a record-tying 99-yard touchdown, giving the Eagles a 23–17 victory.

"All we wanted was a little breathing room," said Quick, who joins five others who have had 99-yarders.

Most yards on a completed pass: 99, Ron Jaworski to Mike Quick, Philadelphia Eagles, vs. Atlanta Falcons, Nov. 10, 1985 (Ties Frank Filchock to Andy Farkas, Washington Redskins, vs. Pittsburgh Steelers, Oct. 15, 1939; George Izo to Bobby Mitchell, Washington Redskins, vs. Cleveland Browns, Sept. 15, 1963; Karl Sweetan to Pat Studstill, Detroit Lions, vs. Baltimore Colts, Oct. 16, 1966; Sonny Jurgensen to Gerry Allen, Washington Redskins, vs. Chicago Bears, Sept. 15, 1968; Jim Plunkett to Cliff Branch, Los Angeles Raiders vs. Washington Redskins, Oct. 2, 1983)

Philadelphia's Mike Quick clicked on a 99-yard pass play in 1985.
Philadelphia Eagles

A Paige in the Book

KANSAS CITY, Mo., Dec. 22, 1985—He's a wide receiver who played at Fresno State but was overlooked in the NFL's 1983 draft. They say it was because he was overshadowed by Henry Ellard, a second-round draft choice of the Los Angeles Rams.

But nobody overshadowed Stephone Paige of the Kansas City Chiefs today when he broke a 40-year-old NFL mark by gaining 309 yards on receptions in the Chiefs' 38–34 defeat of the San Diego Chargers. Playing in pain with bruised ribs that were protected by a flak jacket, Paige caught eight passes, including 84- and 56-yard touchdowns.

Signed as a free agent in 1983, the 6-foot 1-inch, 180-pound Paige capped his finest season with this record performance. His 21.9-yard average per catch was tops in the league.

Most yardage on pass receptions, game: 309, Stephone Paige, Kansas City Chiefs, vs. San Diego Chargers, Dec. 22, 1985

Norwegian Boots

MINNEAPOLIS, Minn., Dec. 22, 1985—A storybook finish called for Jan Stenerud to kick the winning field goal for the Minnesota Vikings today against the Philadelphia Eagles. But the Vikings lost, 37–35, when time ran out as they moved into position for one last 33-yard field-goal attempt.

And so the 43-year-old Norwegian-born Stenerud went into retirement with a record total of 373 field goals over the course of a 19-year career with the Kansas City Chiefs, Green Bay Packers, and the Vikings.

Most field goals, career: 373, Jan Stenerud, Kansas City Chiefs, 1967–79; Green Bay Packers, 1980–83; Minnesota Vikings, 1984–85

The Montana Miracle

SAN FRANCISCO, Cal., Dec. 19, 1986—Capping his remarkable return, Joe Montana quarterbacked the San Francisco 49ers to the NFC Western Division championship tonight in a 24–14 victory over the runner-up Los Angeles Rams.

San Francisco's Joe Montana hands off to Roger Craig.   *Vic Milton*

Montana, who came back into the lineup on Nov. 9 only 55 days after spinal surgery, wound up the regular season by throwing two touchdown passes among his 23 completions (36 attempts, one interception).

His performance enabled Montana to remain at the top for highest completion percentage in a career: 63.16.

Highest completion percentage, career: 63.16, Joe Montana, San Francisco 49ers, 1979–86 (2,878–1818)

Payton's Place

IRVING, Tex., Dec. 21, 1986—Walter Payton of the Chicago Bears injured his right shoulder on his first carry of the game today against the Dallas Cowboys, but that didn't keep him from scoring his 106th career rushing touchdown—tying Jim Brown's all-time NFL record.

With Doug Flutie leading the way at quarterback in place of the injured Jim McMahon, the defending champion Bears won, 24–10, as the regular season ended. Chicago, which scored all its points before the Cowboys got on the scoreboard, had an easier day than the statisticians, who had to work overtime revising Payton's many records.

In his illustrious 12 years as a pro out of Jackson State, Payton has assumed a commanding lead in all-time rushing yardage with 16,193, compared to runner-up Tony Dorsett of Dallas (11,580), and he holds a battery of other marks.

Most touchdowns rushing, career: 106, Walter Payton, Chicago Bears, 1975–86 (ties Jim Brown, Cleveland Browns, 1957–65).
Most yards gained, career: 16,193, Walter Payton, Chicago Bears, 1975–86

Chicago's Walter Payton has charged his way into the record book.

Vic Milton

Most attempts rushing, career: 3,692, Walter Payton, Chicago Bears, 1975–86

Most seasons, 1,000 or more yards rushing: 10, Walter Payton, Chicago Bears, 1975–86

Most yards gained, game: 275, Walter Payton, Chicago Bears, vs. Minnesota Vikings, Nov. 20, 1977

Most games 100 or more yards rushing, career: 77, Walter Payton, Chicago Bears, 1975–86

Most combined net yards, career: 21,053, Walter Payton, Chicago Bears, 1975–86

Soaring Seahawk

SEATTLE, Wash., Dec. 20, 1986—Will the streak ever end for Steve Largent? Perhaps only when he retires. The Seattle Seahawk caught a pass today—actually five of them—to mark the 139th consecutive game in which he's had at least one pass reception.

He did it as the Seahawks, led by Curt Warner's three touchdowns, surprised the AFC Western Division champion Denver Broncos, 41–16, in their regular-season finale.

The Seahawk wide receiver's streak began on Nov. 20, 1977, against the Houston Oilers, and earlier this season, against the San Diego Chargers, he broke the NFL mark of 127 held by Philadelphia's Harold Carmichael (1972–80).

Most consecutive games, pass receptions: 139, Steve Largent, Seattle Seahawks, 1977–86

The Joiner Collection

CLEVELAND, Ohio, Dec. 21, 1986—Although Bernie Kosar and the Cleveland Browns dominated the San Diego Chargers, 47–17, the losers' Charlie Joiner today made two changes in the NFL record book.

The 5-foot 11-inch wide receiver caught three passes for 25 yards, giving him a total of 12,146 yards in his 18-year career. Earlier in the season, he'd broken Dan Maynard's mark of 11,834.

Joiner's three catches extended his NFL lifetime record to 750 receptions.

Most yards, pass receptions, career: 12,146, Charlie Joiner, Houston Oilers, 1969–72; Cincinnati Bengals, 1972–75; San Diego Chargers, 1976–86

Most pass receptions, career: 750, Charlie Joiner, Houston Oilers, 1969–72; Cincinnati Bengals, 1972–75; San Diego Chargers, 1976–86

PRO BASKETBALL

Carom King

PHILADELPHIA, Pa., Nov. 24, 1960—Disappointing a Thanksgiving Day capacity crowd of 11,003 at Convention Hall, the Boston Celtics strengthened their hold on first place by beating the Philadelphia Warriors, 132–129. But you certainly can't fault the Warriors' big Wilt Chamberlain, who hauled down a record 55 rebounds and scored 34 points, despite being guarded by defensive ace Bill Russell. Chamberlain's efforts off the backboards surpassed Russell's NBA record of 51 rebounds grabbed in a game against Syracuse last season.

Most rebounds, game: 55, Wilt Chamberlain, Philadelphia Warriors, vs. Boston Celtics, Nov. 24, 1960

All-Star Boardman

ST. LOUIS, Mo., Jan. 16, 1962—Playing before the hometown fans, Bob Pettit of the St. Louis Hawks pulled down a record 27 rebounds and scored 25 points as he led the West to a 150–130 victory tonight in the NBA All-Star Game. Pettit was chosen Most Valuable Player in this annual game for the fourth time, getting the nod over Wilt Chamberlain, who scored a record 42 points in a losing cause for the East.

Pettit had held both the former rebound record of 26 and the old scoring record of 29 points. The 6-foot 9-inch Hawk forward out of Louisiana State had good support in the West triumph as the Lakers' Elgin Baylor scored 32 points and Jerry West contributed 18. Cincinnati's Oscar Robertson added 26 points for the winners, while Chicago rookie Walt Bellamy scored 23.

Most rebounds, NBA All-Star Game: 27, Bob Pettit, St. Louis Hawks, Jan. 16, 1962
Most points, NBA All-Star Game: 42, Wilt Chamberlain, Philadelphia Warriors, Jan. 16, 1962

A 100 High

HERSHEY, Pa., March 2, 1962—The Big Dipper shone tonight as Wilt Chamberlain rewrote the record book by scoring

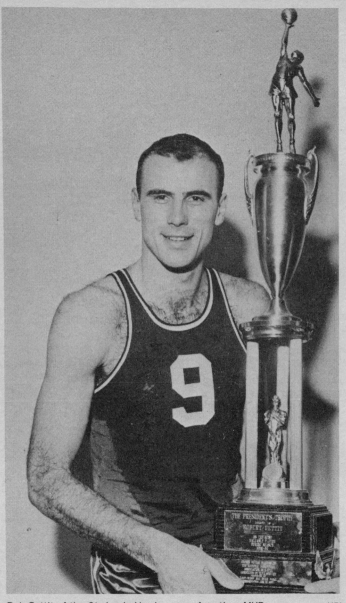
Bob Pettit of the St. Louis Hawks was a four-time MVP.   *UPI*

100 points against the New York Knickerbockers in a regular-season NBA game played here here as one of the Philadelphia Warriors' "home" games.

The 7-foot 1-inch Chamberlain, who attended Overbrook High School in Philadelphia before going to the University of Kansas, established single-game records for most points, most field goals, most free throws made, and most shots, among others.

Chamberlain made his first 10 shots from the charity line and converted on a 28-of-32 overall to go with his 36-for-63 shooting from the field in a game easily won by the Warriors, 169–147.

Despite the defensive efforts of center Darrell Imhoff, forwards Cleveland Buckner and Willie Naulls, and just about everybody else on the Knick team, Chamberlain opened up with 23 points in the first quarter, had 41 at the half, and 69 when the third period ended. In the fourth quarter his teammates began feeding him consistently so that he could break his own record of 78 points scored earlier this season. The final two points came on a dunk shot with 46 seconds remaining in the game.

Most points, game: 100, Wilt Chamberlain, Philadelphia Warriors, vs. New York Knickerbockers, March 2, 1962

Most field goals attempted, game: 63, Wilt Chamberlain, Philadelphia Warriors, vs. New York Knickerbockers, March 2, 1962

Most field goals made, game: 36, Wilt Chamberlain, Philadelphia Warriors, vs. N.Y. Knickerbockers, March 2, 1962

Most free throws made, game: 28, Wilt Chamberlain, Philadelphia Warriors, vs. N.Y. Knickerbockers, March 2, 1962

Most points, half: 59, Wilt Chamberlain, Philadelphia Warriors, vs. N.Y. Knickerbockers, March 2, 1962

Making a Point

CHICAGO, Ill., March 14, 1962—Wilt Chamberlain, who set a rebounding record last season, finished this year with a 34-point performance that gave him 4,029 points and a 50.4-point-per-game scoring average as he led the Philadelphia Warriors to a 119–115 decision today over the expansion Chicago Packers.

The 7-foot Chamberlain, who created the NBA record of 2,149 rebounds during the 1960–61 campaign, was a scoring phenom this year as he set records for the most field goal attempts, most field goals made, most free throws attempted, in addition to his total points and scoring average. In one game this year, against the New York Knicks, he scored a record high 100 points.

Most points, season: 4,029, Wilt Chamberlain, Philadelphia Warriors, 1961–62

Highest scoring average, season: 50.4, Wilt Chamberlain, Philadelphia Warriors, 1961–62

Most field goals attempted, season: 3,159, Wilt Chamberlain, Philadelphia Warriors, 1961–62

Most field goals made, season: 1,597, Wilt Chamberlain, Philadelphia Warriors, 1961–62

Most free throws attempted, season: 1,363, Wilt Chamberlain, Philadelphia Warriors, 1961–62

Most rebounds, season: 2,149, Wilt Chamberlain, Philadelphia Warriors, 1960–61

Sweet Charity

LOS ANGELES, Cal., March 20, 1966—Jerry West converted 11 of 12 free throws as he scored 35 points in leading Los Angeles to a 124–112 victory over the San Francisco Warriors tonight. The loss prevented the Warriors from gaining a playoff berth in the NBA's Western Division.

The 6-foot 3-inch West, a six-year pro out of West Virginia University, created an NBA record with his free-throw shooting. The 11 tonight raised his total for the season to 840, breaking the old mark of 835 set by Wilt Chamberlain four seasons ago. West, who is called "Zeke from Cabin Creek," averaged 28.7 points a game this season.

Most free throws made, season: 840, Jerry West, Los Angeles Lakers, 1965–66

Deadly

SYRACUSE, N.Y., Feb. 28, 1967—Wilt Chamberlain made his first four shots from the floor before he missed a whirling underhanded layup, ending a record 35-for-35 field-goal shooting streak. Wilt went on to score 28 points tonight in leading the Philadelphia 76ers past Cincinnati, 127–107. The 76ers played in this upstate New York city for 15 seasons as the Syracuse Nationals before transferring to Philadelphia four years ago.

Los Angeles's Jerry West lines up his 840th successful free throw, a single-season standard. *UPI*

Chamberlain's shooting streak began 11 days ago against this same Cincinnati team in a 127–118 Philadelphia victory in Cleveland. The highlight of the streak, however, came a week ago when the Big Dipper dropped in 11 shots in 11 attempts in taking the 76ers to a 123–122 victory over St. Louis.

Most consecutive field goals: 35, Wilt Chamberlain, Philadelphia 76ers, Feb. 17, 1967, to Feb. 28, 1967

End of Laker Chain

MILWAUKEE, Wis., Jan. 9, 1972—The team defense of the Milwaukee Bucks and the individual brilliance of Kareem Abdul-Jabbar brought an end to the longest winning streak in major professional sports. Milwaukee defeated the Los Angeles Lakers, 120–104, before a sellout crowd of 10,746 and a national television audience this afternoon, ending the Lakers' 33-game winning streak.

The string of victories included at least one triumph over every other team in the league, including these same Bucks. The Lakers' effort, which began October 31, was the longest winning streak compiled by a major league team in basketball, football, baseball, or hockey.

The defeat came about because Milwaukee guards Lucius Allen, Oscar Robertson, Jon McGlocklin, and Wali Jones kept rushing back on defense, cutting off the Lakers' fast break. Los Angeles had used the rebounding of Wilt Chamberlain and Happy Hairston and the quickness of Jerry West, Gail Goodrich, Jim Price, and Jim McMillian to run their way to victory in most of the 33 triumphs.

In addition to the defense by the Buck backcourt, Milwaukee center Kareem Abdul-Jabbar, the former Lew Alcindor, outplayed Chamberlain in the pivot and outfought Hairston under the boards as he scored 39 points and pulled 20 rebounds.

Most consecutive victories: 33, Los Angeles Lakers, Oct. 31, 1971, to Jan. 7, 1972

The Last Dip

OAKLAND, Cal., March 25, 1973—Wilt Chamberlain, who apparently can do anything he wants to do with a basketball

Milwaukee's Kareem Abdul-Jabbar lofts one over Wilt Chamberlain as the Bucks end the Lakers' 33-game winning streak.   *UPI*

when he puts his mind to it, took his first shot at the basket in 75 minutes of playing time over a two-game span. It was his only shot of the night, and he missed it, but the Los Angeles Lakers won this final game of the season over the Golden State Warriors, 96–89.

The Big Dipper, playing the last regular-season game of his career, scored one point on a free throw, pulled down 18 rebounds, and passed for nine assists. In his next-to-last game, against the Milwaukee Bucks, Chamberlain failed to take any shots at all from the field.

Throughout his career, the 7-foot 1-inch center has been something of a puzzle, although no one has ever questioned his ability. After leading the league in scoring and becoming MVP in his first year, 1959–60, with the Philadelphia Warriors, Chamberlain followed the next season by setting a mark for rebounds (2,149) that still stands. In 1961–62 he shattered all sorts of records en route to a 14-year career that included championships with the Philadelphia 76ers in 1967 and the Lakers in 1972.

Among his many achievements, Wilt Chamberlain never fouled out of a game.
UPI

He owns many of the league's career offensive records, among other marks, and he has the added distinction of never having fouled out of a game.

Most seasons and most consecutive seasons leading league in scoring: 7, Wilt Chamberlain, Philadelphia Warriors, 1959–62; San Francisco Warriors, 1962–64; San Francisco Warriors–Philadelphia 76ers, 1964–65; Philadelphia 76ers, 1965–66
Highest average, points per game, career (minimum 400 games): 30.1, Philadelphia Warriors, 1959–62; San Francisco Warriors, 1962–64; San Francisco Warriors–Philadelphia 76ers, 1964–65; Philadelphia 76ers, 1965–68; Los Angeles Lakers, 1968–73
Most games, 50 or more points, career: 118, Wilt Chamberlain, Philadelphia Warriors, 1959–62; San Francisco Warriors, 1962–64; San Francisco Warriors–Philadelphia 76ers, 1964–65; Philadelphia 76ers, 1965–68; Los Angeles Lakers, 1968–73
Most seasons and most consecutive seasons leading league in field goals: 9, Wilt Chamberlain, Philadelphia Warriors, 1960–61; San Francisco Warriors, 1962–64; San Francisco Warriors–Philadelphia 76ers, 1964–65; Philadelphia 76ers, 1965–66
Most seasons leading league in rebounds: 11, Wilt Chamberlain, Philadelphia Warriors, 1959–60, 1961–62; San Francisco Warriors, 1965–66, 1967–68; Los Angeles Lakers, 1968–69, 1970–71, 1972–73
Most rebounds, career: 23,924, Wilt Chamberlain, Philadelphia Warriors, 1959–62; San Francisco Warriors, 1962–65; Philadelphia 76ers, 1964–68; Los Angeles Lakers, 1968–73

Oscar Performance

MILWAUKEE, Wis., March 26, 1974—It was Oscar Robertson Night at the Milwaukee Arena and a full house was on hand to pay tribute to the greatest playmaker in NBA history.

Robertson, troubled by nagging injuries much of the season, made four field goals, converted six of six from the free-throw line, and made nine assists as the Milwaukee Bucks routed Kansas City-Omaha, 118–98. The six free throws gave Robertson 7,694 for his career, while the assists raised his pro total to 9,887, both NBA records.

The 6-foot 5-inch Robertson, who never played on a national championship team in college nor on an NBA champion until he came to Milwaukee four years ago, finished his career with 26,710 points, second on the all-time list behind Wilt Chamberlain.

Oscar Robertson's helping hand accounted for a record 9,887 assists.

Most assists, career: 9,887, Oscar Robertson, Cincinnati Royals, 1960–70,
  Milwaukee Bucks, 1970–74
Most free throws made, career: 7,694, Oscar Robertson, Cincinnati
  Royals, 1960–70; Milwaukee Bucks, 1970–74

West Is Best

INGLEWOOD, Cal., April 2, 1974—It wasn't much of a performance, not by Jerry West's standards. But the veteran Los Angeles Laker guard came off the bench tonight to play for 14 minutes and inspire his teammates, bringing the Lakers their first victory in three playoff games with the Milwaukee Bucks, 98–96, before a capacity crowd of 17,505 in the Forum.

Laker Jerry West had the highest per-game average in NBA playoff history.
Malcolm Emmons

Elmore Smith was the real star of the game, scoring 30 points and hauling down 17 rebounds as he outplayed Milwaukee's Kareem Abdul-Jabbar, who finished with 29 points and 15 rebounds.

But it was West who provided the lift the Lakers needed. Sidelined since February 5 with a pulled abdominal muscle, West entered the game in the second quarter to a standing ovation. This—plus West's hitting on his first jump shot—provided the spark. Jerry's totals were a mere four points, two rebounds, and an assist.

It was, as it turned out, his final appearance in a distinguished 13-year career. His 29.1-point-per-game average and 1,213 successful free throws in the playoffs are NBA records.

Highest per-game scoring average, NBA playoffs: 29.1 (4,457 points in 153 games), Jerry West, Los Angeles Lakers, 1960–74

Most free throws made, NBA playoffs: 1,213, Jerry West, Los Angeles Lakers, 1960–74

Buckets by the Bushel

SAN DIEGO, Cal., Feb. 14, 1975—It wasn't exactly a St. Valentine's Day massacre, but there was shooting aplenty tonight as the San Diego Conquistadors and the New York Nets took four overtimes to decide a winner. San Diego finally took the American Baskeball Association contest, 176–166.

Along the way, the two teams scored more points than any other opponents in pro basketball history, played the longest game in ABA annals (one NBA game lasted six overtimes in 1951 before the advent of the 24-second clock) and established countless league and club records. Almost lost in the welter of figures was a 63-point scoring performance by the Nets' Dr. J., Julius Erving, a personal high for him and one of the highest totals in pro history.

The Conquistadors, or Q's, as they are usually called, played like anything but the last-place team they are by getting clutch shooting from Travis Grant, Bo Lamar, and Warren Jabali as they came from behind and prolonged the game. In the extra periods the Nets, defending league champion and currently on top of the Eastern Division standings, used outside accuracy by Billy Melchionni and Brian Taylor to keep alive.

The game took three hours and ten minutes to complete before a crowd of 2,916. Not everyone stayed until the end.

Most points scored, both teams, one game: 342, San Diego Conquistadors (176) vs. New York Nets (166), Feb. 14, 1975

The New York Nets' Julius Erving hit for 63 points in the longest game, against the San Diego Conquistadors. *San Diego Union*

Longest Shot

SAN ANTONIO, Tex., Jan. 19, 1977—It happened late in the first half of the game tonight between the Chicago Bulls and the San Antonio Spurs.

Artis Gilmore gathered in a rebound for Chicago and handed off to Norm Van Lier, who was under the basket. Van Lier uncorked a hook shot that traveled the length of the court and swished through the basket. It was measured as an 84-footer, the longest basket in NBA history.

Ironically, those were Van Lier's only two points of the night as the Bulls were beaten by the Spurs, 115–107.

Longest basket: 84 feet, Norm Van Lier, Chicago Bulls, Jan. 19, 1977

A Porter's Job

EAST RUTHERFORD, N.J., Feb. 24, 1978—Kevin Porter gave a course tonight in the art of feeding as the New Jersey Nets downed the Houston Rockets, 126–112.

The 5-foot 11-inch guard collected 29 assists for an NBA single-game record. He scored 14 points, leaving the big numbers in that department to John Williamson, 39, and Bernard King, 35.

Porter's 29 assists broke the mark of 28 that had been shared by Bob Cousy of the Boston Celtics and Guy Rodgers of the San Francisco Warriors.

Most assists, game: 29, Kevin Porter, New Jersey Nets, Feb. 24, 1978

Pure Calvin

SAN ANTONIO, Tex., March 29, 1981—Although San Antonio defeated Houston, 135–109, tonight, there was a high note sounded for little Calvin Murphy of the Rockets. His 4-for-4 from the free-throw line enabled him to finish the season with a .958 free-throw percentage, an NBA record.

The 5-foot 9-inch Murphy, one of the finest pure shooters in the game, set another NBA mark early in the season when he registered 78 consecutive free throws.

Houston's Calvin Murphy is a little guy who stood tall on the free-throw
line and elsewhere.

Ron Modra

Highest free-throw percentage, season: .958, Calvin Murphy, Houston, 1980–81
Most consecutive free throws made, season: 78, Calvin Murphy, Houston, Dec. 27, 1980—Feb. 28, 1981

A Smithian Streak

DALLAS, Tex., March 13, 1983—He got to play only four minutes in the second half and went 2-for-2 for four points today as the Dallas Mavericks beat the San Diego Clippers, 111–102.

For Randy Smith, the durable Clipper guard, it was an insignificant finale to a monumental streak that had begun when he was with the Buffalo Braves on Feb. 18, 1972. Since then, playing for the Braves, the Clippers, the Cleveland Cavaliers, the New York Knickerbockers, and the Clippers once more, Smith never missed a game.

It all added up to 906 consecutive games, an NBA record, and it ended when Smith was given his release.

Although Smith's is the NBA standard, Ron Boone can lay claim to the longest all-time pro mark. Boone, a guard who played for six teams in the American Basketball Association and NBA, appeared in 1,041 consecutive games from 1968 to 1981.

Most consecutive games played, NBA: 906, Randy Smith, Buffalo Braves, San Diego Clippers, Cleveland Cavaliers, New York Knickerbockers, San Diego Clippers, Feb. 18, 1972—March 13, 1983
Most consecutive games played, ABA-NBA: 1,041, Ron Boone, Dallas Chapparrals, Utah Stars, St. Louis Spirits, Kansas City Kings, Los Angeles Lakers, Utah Jazz, Oct. 31, 1968—Jan. 24, 1981

Best Bet

LAS VEGAS, Nev., Jan. 4, 1984—Even in this betting capital of the world there were no odds given for Adrian Dantley's chances of breaking Wilt Chamberlain's NBA mark of 28 free throws made in one game.

Well, the Utah Jazz's star forward didn't break it tonight; he tied it. Of his 46 points in the 116–111 victory over the Houston Rockets, Dantley scored 28 on fouls. He missed only one foul shot, the difference between tying and snapping Chamberlain's 22-year-old record.

"The Big E"

KANSAS CITY, Mo., April 14, 1984—Fittingly, Elvin Hayes of the Houston Rockets had four personal fouls tonight as he played the final game of his 16-year career against the Kansas City Kings, who prevailed, 108–96.

Elvin Hayes delivered at many specialties in the course of 16 years in the NBA.   *Houston Rockets*

Thus the 6-foot 9-inch, 235-pound forward finished with a career-record total of 4,193 fouls, an indication of his aggressive play but not the only commentary on a distinguished performer known for his shooting skills and leaping ability for rebounds.

Hayes, whose final seasons were in the city where he gained fame as a University of Houston standout, had a 21-point career average, and he played exactly 50,000 minutes.

Most personal fouls, career: 4,193, Elvin Hayes, San Diego Rockets, 1968–71; Houston Rockets, 1971–72; Baltimore Bullets, 1972–73; Capital Bullets, 1973–74; Washington Bullets, 1974–81; Houston Rockets, 1981–84

Magic's Magic

LOS ANGELES, Cal., May 15, 1984—Magic Johnson broke a playoff record with 24 assists tonight as the Los Angeles Lakers downed the Phoenix Suns, 118–102, in the Western Conference playoffs.

Magic attempted only five shots, making two of them, while he concentrated on feeding his teammates, seven of whom were in double figures. Kareem Abdul-Jabbar's 21 points were high for the Lakers, who took a 2-0 lead in the series.

The 6-foot 9-inch Laker guard broke the playoff record of 20 assists made by Johnny Moore of the San Antonio Spurs against Denver last year.

Most assists, playoffs, game: 24, Magic Johnson, Los Angeles Lakers, vs. Phoenix Suns, May 15, 1984

The Lakers' Magic Johnson is always ready for the assist and whatever magic is needed.   *Ira Golden*

Bird's Series Swoop

BOSTON, Mass., June 12, 1984—Larry Bird, MVP of the regular season, added playoff MVP laurels tonight as the Boston Celtics defeated the Los Angeles Lakers, 111–102, for their 15th NBA championship.

In the seventh and deciding game, Bird scored 20 points, hauled in 12 rebounds and had 2 steals, giving him a record total of 15 steals for a seven-game championship series.

The 6-foot 9-inch, 220-pound forward was the series' leading scorer with 192 points, a 27.4-point average, a high of 34 points in the fifth game.

Most steals, championship series, seven games: 15, Larry Bird, Boston Celtics, vs. Los Angeles Lakers, 1984

The Celtics' Larry Bird is, among other things, the greatest stealer in NBA championship playoff history.   *Wide World*

"The Mad Bomber"

SAN ANTONIO, Tex., April 14, 1985—He was known at Louisville University for his rip-roaring slam dunks, but now he makes a living drilling three-point shots as "The Mad Bomber" of the Utah Jazz.

Darrell Griffith, a 6-foot 4-inch, 190-pound guard, scored one tonight to give him a record 92 for the season as the Seattle SuperSonics edged the Jazz, 119–118.

Nobody has made as many attempts at three-pointers in a career (745) as Griffith, but he doesn't own all the records in this specialty. The Houston Oilers' Rick Barry and the Denver Nuggets' John Roche share the one-game high with eight. And Scott Wedman of the Boston Celtics shot a record 11 consecutive three-pointers.

Most three-point field goal attempts, career: 745, Darrell Griffith, Utah Jazz, 1980–85

Most three-point field goals, season: 92, Darrell Griffith, Utah Jazz, 1984–85

Most three-point field goal attempts, season: 257, Darrell Griffith, Utah Jazz, 1984–85

*As of start of 1986–87 season.

Utah's Darrell Griffith is master of the three-point bomb.   *Utah Jazz*

Detroit's Isiah Thomas operates on all pistons and is a wheeler and
dealer in assists.   *Ira Golden*

Led by Isiah

CLEVELAND, Ohio, April 14, 1985—Whatever else he did in
the regular season that ended today with Detroit defeating
Cleveland, 116–113, Isiah Thomas could at least lay claim to
two NBA records.

The four-year Piston guard out of Indiana finished with 1,123
assists, the most ever in a season, and a 13.9 assists-per-game
average, highest in history.

He erased the 1,099 and 13.4 marks set by another Piston, Kevin Porter, in 1978–79.

Most assists, season: 1,123, Isiah Thomas, Detroit Pistons, 1984–85
Highest average, assists per game, season: 13.9, Isiah Thomas, Detroit Pistons, 1984–85

Great Scott!

BOSTON, Mass., May 27, 1985—Scott Wedman, the 11-year pro veteran who serves as a swingman for the Boston Celtics, had the shooting day of a lifetime today as the Celtics routed the Los Angeles Lakers, 148–114, in the opening game of the championship series.

Wedman hit 11-for-11 from the floor, including four three-pointers—three in succession—to set an NBA playoff record.

The 33-year-old Wedman, a product of Colorado University who played for seven years with the Kansas City Kings, then with the Cleveland Cavaliers before joining the Celtics in 1982–83, registered a total of 26 points, which tied teammate Kevin McHale for scoring honors. He played 23 minutes.

His perfect shooting was also a new goal-percentage mark (1.000), breaking the playoff record of .917 previously shared by Bill Bradley of the New York Knickerbockers and James Worthy of the Los Angeles Lakers.

Most consecutive field goals, game, championship series: 11, Scott Wedman, Boston Celtics, May 27, 1985
Highest field-goal percentage, game, championship series (minimum 8 field goals): 1.000, Scott Wedman, Boston Celtics, May 27, 1985

Kareem's Lot

LOS ANGELES, Cal., April 10, 1986—He's 39 years old and is still regarded as the most potent offensive force in pro basketball.

Kareem Abdul-Jabbar of the Los Angeles Lakers, bothered by a respiratory infection that would end his regular season tonight, played 36 minutes and scored 23 points as the Pacific Division champion Lakers downed the Midwest Division champion Houston Rockets, 117–113.

The Laker's Kareem Abdul-Jabbar, in the twilight of his career, holds a bushel of records.
Ira Golden

After 17 seasons, with the Milwaukee Bucks starting in 1976–70, when he was still known as Lew Alcindor, and then with the Lakers, the 7-foot 2-inch, 235-pound center stands tall with NBA career records for games played (1,328), minutes played (51,002), points scored (35,108), and most field goals (14,484), among other marks.

*Most games, career: 1,328, Kareem Abdul-Jabbar, Milwaukee Bucks, 1969–75; Los Angeles Lakers, 1975–86
*Most minutes, career: 51,002, Kareem Abdul-Jabbar, Milwaukee Bucks, 1969–75; Los Angeles Lakers, 1975–86
*Most points scored, career: 35,108, Kareem Abdul-Jabbar, Milwaukee Bucks, 1969–75; Los Angeles Lakers, 1975–86
*Most field goals, career: 14,484, Kareem Abdul-Jabbar, Milwaukee Bucks, 1969–75; Los Angeles Lakers, 1975–86

*As of start of 1986–87 season.

Here Comes Mr. Jordan

BOSTON, Mass., April 20, 1986—Michael Jordan, the air-borne sensation of the Chicago Bulls, scored a playoff-record 63 points today against the Boston Celtics.

Despite his heroics, the Celtics won in double overtime, 135–131, to give them a 2–0 advantage in the opening-round series.

Jordan, the 6-foot 6-inch leaping lizard out of North Carolina, hit on 22 of 41 shots from the field and made 19 of his 21 attempts from the foul line.

He broke Elgin Baylor's playoff mark of 61, set by the Los Angeles Laker against the Celtics in the 1962 championship series.

Most points, NBA playoffs, game: 63, Michael Jordan, Chicago Bulls, vs. Boston Celtics, April 20, 1986

The Bulls' Michael Jordan soared into the record book in the 1986 playoffs.
Chicago Bulls

HOCKEY

Goal-Getter

QUEBEC CITY, Quebec, Jan. 31, 1920—Joe Malone, who led the National Hockey League in scoring in its first season a couple of years ago with 44 goals in 20 games, has another line in the record book. The new Quebec Bulldog, who came from the Montreal Canadiens at the beginning of the season, scored seven goals tonight against the Toronto St. Patricks, more goals than anyone has ever scored in a single NHL game. The Bulldogs beat Toronto, 10–6.

Most goals, game: 7, Joe Malone, Quebec Bulldogs, vs. Toronto St. Patricks, Jan. 31, 1920

Former Canadien Joe Malone scored seven goals for the Quebec Bulldogs against the Toronto St. Pats.　　　*Hockey Hall of Fame*

Canadien Goose Eggs

MONTREAL, Quebec, March 14, 1929—Montreal Canadien goalie George Hainsworth recorded his 22nd shutout in 44 games as he held the Maroons scoreless in tonight's season closer. Howie Morenz scored the only goal as the Canadiens beat their intra-city rivals, 1–0.

Hainsworth's phenomenal goaltending—he allowed only 43 goals all season—is all the more surprising in view of a rule change implemented by the NHL this season that was supposed to introduce more offense into the game. The change allowed forward passing in all three zones, a team's defensive zone, the center zone between the blue lines,* and in the attacking zone. Previously, no forward passing was allowed in the attacking zone.

Most shutouts, season: 22, George Hainsworth, Montreal Canadiens, 1928–29

*Editor's Note: The red line at center ice was not introduced until 1943.

Puck Stopper

NEW YORK, Feb. 1, 1970—Filling in for the injured Ed Giacomin, 40-year-old Terry Sawchuk was minding the nets for the New York Rangers tonight and he stopped 29 Pittsburgh shots to chalk up the 103rd shutout of his National Hockey League career, as New York won, 6–0.

It was a memorable night on the Madison Square Garden ice as the Rangers' Dave Balon scored three goals for his first hat trick and Billy Fairbairn recorded three assists to establish a club scoring mark of 42 points by a rookie.

But the hero of the night was Sawchuk, Rookie of the Year 21 seasons ago, the only man ever to shut out more than 100 opposing teams. He did it with Detroit, the team he broke in with in 1949, Boston, Toronto, Los Angeles, and the Rangers. This was Sawchuk's first shutout since the 1967–68 season, when he was with the Kings.

Most shutouts, NHL career: 103, Terry Sawchuk, Detroit Red Wings, 1949–55; Boston Bruins, 1955–57; Detroit Red Wings, 1957–64; Toronto Maple Leafs, 1964–67; Los Angeles Kings, 1967–68; Detroit Red Wings, 1968–69; New York Rangers, 1969–70

Terry Sawchuck recorded his 103rd shutout playing with the New York Rangers.   *UPI*

Tony Awards

CHICAGO, Ill., March 29, 1970—Squat, but mobile, Tony Esposito recorded the 15th shutout of this, his rookie season, as the Chicago Black Hawks beat the Toronto Maple Leafs tonight, 4–0. Three days ago Esposito broke Harry Lumley's 16-year-old modern record with his 14th shutout of the season.

The modern era for goaltenders dates from the 1943–44 season when the red line at center ice was introduced. This line had the effect of speeding up the game by adding more offense since it allowed a player to pass the puck out of his own defensive zone. Previously the player would have to carry the puck out of the zone himself.

Nearing the end of a spectacular season, Esposito—whose brother Phil is a leading scorer with the Boston Bruins—should win both the Calder Trophy as Rookie of the Year and the Vezina Trophy as the league's best goaltender.

Most shutouts, season (modern): 15, Tony Esposito, Chicago Black Hawks, 1969–70

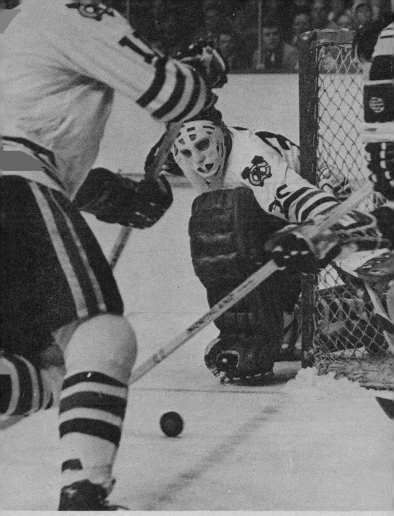

Tony Esposito set the modern mark of 15 shutouts in a season as a
Black Hawks' rookie.   *Dick Raphael*

Flyers' Hammer

PHILADELPHIA, Pa., April 6, 1975—The Philadelphia Flyers' Hammer struck in an unusual manner tonight, scoring a goal and waiting until only eight minutes remained in the game before getting into a fight. The Hammer, as forward Dave Schultz is referred to by his Flyer teammates, scored a third-period goal—his ninth goal of the season—in helping Philadelphia to a 6–2 victory over Atlanta in the last game of the regular season.

Eight minutes after scoring, Schultz and Ed Kea of the Flames were engaging in fisticuffs and were sent to the penalty box with major and minor penalties, much to the delight of the 17,007 fans in the Spectrum, who have learned to love the Hammer's roughhouse tactics. The seven penalty minutes tonight gave Schultz a total of 472 for the season, far outdistancing the record 348 penalty minutes he accumulated last year in leading Philadelphia to the Stanley Cup championship.

Most penalty minutes, season: 472, Dave Schultz, Philadelphia Flyers, 1974–75

Sittler's Explosion

TORONTO, Ont., Feb. 7, 1976—Until tonight, Darryl Sittler was in a slump, having scored only five goals in the last 17 games. But the Toronto Maple Leaf center exploded tonight with six goals (on 10 shots) and four assists in an 11–4 thumping of the Boston Bruins.

His 10 points smashed the one-game NHL mark set by Maurice "Rocket" Richard of the Montreal Canadiens in 1944 (five goals and three assists).

Most points, game: 10, Darryl Sittler, Toronto Maple Leafs, vs. Boston Bruins, Feb. 7, 1976 (six goals, four assists)

Marathon Man

ATLANTA, Ga., Dec. 21, 1979—When he isn't playing hockey, Garry Unger rides horses and motorcycles. Injuries notwithstanding, he hasn't missed a game in more than 11 seasons.

Philadelphia's Dave Schultz and his big stick added up to record penalties.

Tonight the 5-foot 11-inch, 170-pound forward of the Atlanta Flames made it 914 consecutive games as the St. Louis Blues downed the Flames, 5–1.

In 1975–76, playing for the Blues, Unger broke the previous record of 630 games set by Andy Hebenton with the New York Rangers and Boston Bruins.

Most consecutive games: 914, Garry Unger, Toronto Maple Leafs, Detroit Red Wings, St. Louis Blues, Atlanta Flames, Feb. 4, 1968—Dec. 21, 1979

In the Penalty Box

PHILADELPHIA, Pa., March 11, 1979—In a brawl-filled, record-breaking match, the Philadelphia Flyers tonight outpunched the Los Angeles Kings, 6–3.

Kings' defenseman Randy Holt set a game and period record for most penalty minutes, 67, all in the first period, with one minor, three majors, two 10-minute misconducts, and three game misconducts.

The Flyers and Kings also set a mark for most penalty minutes in a period (372), and the Flyers posted a record for most penalty minutes by one team in a period (188).

Most penalty minutes, game, period: 67, Randy Holt, Los Angeles Kings, March 11, 1979
Most penalty minutes, both teams, one period: 372, Philadelphia Flyers (188), Los Angeles Kings (184), March 11, 1979
Most penalty minutes, one team, one period: 188, Philadelphia Flyers, vs. Los Angeles Kings, March 11, 1979

Here's Howe

HARTFORD, Conn., April 6, 1980—Fifty-two-year-old Gordie Howe ended his regular-season career tonight with a goal and an assist as the Hartford Whalers topped the Detroit Red Wings, 5–3.

In his 26th NHL season (there were six others in the World Hockey Association) the remarkable Methuselah of hockey added to a legend that had begun with the Detroit Red Wings in 1946–47.

Gordie Howe ended his 26-year NHL career with the Hartford Whalers and with a barrel of records.   *Wide World*

He ended up with NHL career records for most seasons (26), most games (1,767), most goals (801), most assists (1,049), and most points (1,850), among others.

Most seasons: 26, Gordie Howe, Detroit Red Wings, 1946–71; Hartford Whalers, 1979–80

Most goals: 801, Gordie Howe, Detroit Red Wings, 1946–71; Hartford Whalers, 1979–80

Most assists: 1,049, Gordie Howe, Detroit Red Wings, 1946–71; Hartford Whalers, 1979–80

Most points: 1,850, Gordie Howe, Detroit Red Wings, 1946–71; Hartford Whalers, 1979–80

146

The Mark of a Tiger

LOS ANGELES, Cal., April 5, 1986—For good reason his nickname is "Tiger." Dave Williams of the Los Angeles Kings, the most penalized player in NHL history, had only one penalty today as the Vancouver Canucks bested the Kings, 5–3. But he finished the season with a record career total of 3,515 minutes in the penalty box, not including the playoffs.

The 5-foot 11-inch, 190-pound left wing has made his mark over 12 seasons with four teams.

Most penalty minutes, career: 3,515, Dave Williams, Toronto Maple Leafs, Vancouver Canucks, Detroit Red Wings, Los Angeles Kings, 1974–86

*As of start of 1986–87 season.

The Great Gretzky

VANCOUVER, B.C., April 6, 1986—Although Wayne Gretzky's contribution was a lone assist today, it added to his record-

The likeliest candidate to break the season marks of Edmonton's Wayne Gretzky is Wayne Gretzky.   *Richard Pilling*

smashing year as the Edmonton Oilers edged the Vancouver Canucks, 3–2.

The Great Gretzky wound up the regular season with a record 163 assists and a total of 215 points, the most in NHL history.

Among his many other marks, the 26-year-old center has the most goals in a season (92), and he shares the record for most assists in a game (seven).

Most goals, season: 92, Wayne Gretzky, Edmonton Oilers, 1981–82
Most assists, season: 163, Wayne Gretzky, Edmonton Oilers, 1985–86
Most points, season: 215, Wayne Gretzky, Edmonton Oilers, 1985–86
Most assists, game: 7, Wayne Gretzky, Edmonton Oilers, vs. Washington Capitals, Feb. 15, 1980 (Ties Billy Taylor, Detroit Red Wings, vs. Chicago Black Hawks, March 16, 1947)

BOXING

Moore Knockouts

PHOENIX, Ariz., March 15, 1963—Former light heavyweight champion Archie Moore "unretired" tonight to pound professional wrestler Mike DiBiase for two rounds and 29 seconds before the fight was called, a technical knockout.

The 50-year-old Moore, who has been boxing for 28 years, had his first knockout in his first professional fight in Hot Springs, Ark., against the Poco Kid, Moore has more knockouts to his credit than any other man who stepped into the ring, but exactly how many—like his date of birth—is a point of contention. *Ring Magazine Encyclopedia*, which does not differentiate between knockouts and technical knockouts, credits Moore with 140.

Accuracy with numbers has never bothered Moore, who won his light heavyweight title from Joey Maxim in 1952. He claims Dec. 13, 1916, as his birthday, but his mother maintained Archibald Lee Wright was born in 1913 in Benoit, Miss.

Most knockouts, professional career: 140, Archie Moore, 1935–63

Boxing's knockout king, Archie Moore, won the light heavyweight title from Joey Maxim in 1952. *UPI*

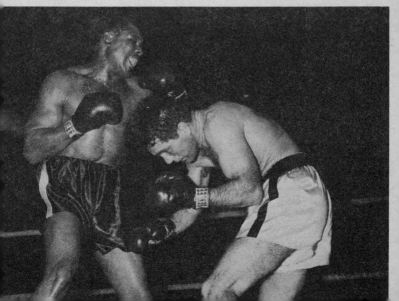

En route to the heavyweight crown, Rocky Marciano knocked out former heavyweight champ Joe Louis.
UPI

The Brockton Blockbuster

NEWTON, Iowa, Aug. 31, 1969—Rocky Marciano planned to celebrate his 46th birthday tomorrow at a party in Des Moines, Iowa. But the former world heavyweight champion was killed here with two others last night in a crash of a single-engine Cessna 172. He was en route from Chicago.

The Brockton Blockbuster won all 49 of his professional fights—43 by knockouts—before announcing his retirement in 1956. He came out of Brockton, Mass., where his father was a shoemaker, and he won the heavyweight title by knocking out Jersey Joe Walcott in 1952. During a three-and-a-half-year reign he defended his title six times, the last when he knocked out Archie Moore in 1955.

A rugged puncher, Marciano was counted among the best of the all-time heavyweights—in a class that included Jack Dempsey, Gene Tunney, and Joe Louis, the latter one of Marciano's knockout victims.

The only heavyweight champion without a loss or a draw over an entire career: Rocky Marciano, 49-for-49, March 17, 1947–Sept. 21, 1955

Ali's Triple

NEW ORLEANS, La., Sept. 15, 1978—It happened at the end of the seventh round. After landing two solid punches, 36-year-old Muhammad Ali ducked under a wild swing by heavyweight champion Leon Spinks as the bell sounded. Heading back to his corner, Ali went into his familiar dance, the Ali Shuffle. And the crowd of 70,000 at the Superdome cheered wildly. The old Ali was back.

Eight rounds later, it was all over. Ali, winner by unanimous decision, had captured the world championship for a record third time.

He'd knocked out Sonny Liston in 1964 for his first title, he'd knocked out George Foreman in 1974 to win the title for the second time, and now he'd lifted the crown from the 25-year-old Spinks, who had dethroned him seven months ago. Spinks wound up with the dubious distinction of having held the heavyweight title for the shortest time in history.

And once more Ali was the greatest.

Most times heavyweight champion: 3, Muhammad Ali, vs. Sonny Liston, KO7, Feb. 25, 1964; vs. George Foreman, K08, Oct. 30, 1974; vs. Leon Spinks, W15, Sept. 15, 1978

Muhammad Ali regained the heavyweight title he'd lost to Leon Spinks by scoring a decision over Spinks in 1978.   *Wide World*

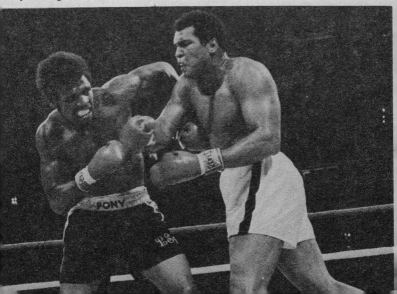

COLLEGE FOOTBALL

Army's Glenn Davis (right) set his college rushing mark playing with Doc Blanchard (center) and being coached by Red Blaik. *UPI*

Mr. Inside and Mr. Outside

PHILADELPHIA, Pa., Nov. 30, 1946—The greatest era in Army football came to an end today as Mr. Inside and Mr. Outside played in their last collegiate game together. And it was almost a disaster. The Cadets, undefeated in three years (one scoreless tie with Notre Dame to blemish the slate) were saved by the clock. Navy, loser of seven straight after an opening-game victory, was in possession of the ball on the Army three-yard line, trailing 21–18 when the final gun sounded.

The crowd of 100,000, including President Harry S. Truman, had watched the Cadets open up a 21–6 halftime lead with Mr. Inside, Doc Blanchard, scoring twice and Mr. Outside, Glenn Davis, picking up the other touchdown. The score by Davis, on a 13-yard run after a pitchout from Arnie Tucker, was the 59th of his varsity career, giving him 354 points. Before the day was out, Davis gained his 2,957th yard rushing for a record average of 8.26 yards per carry.

But nobody was thinking much about records in the second half of the game as Reeves Baysinger, Bill Hawkins, and Leon

157

Bramlett sparked the Middies to what would have been the greatest upset in the Army-Navy series.

Highest rushing average, major college career (minimum 300 attempts): 8.26 yards per carry (358 rushes for 2,957 yards), Glenn Davis, Army, 1943–46

Mississippi Showboat

STARKVILLE, Miss., Dec. 1, 1951—Although he had scored only three touchdowns all season, Arnold "Showboat" Boykin lived up to his nickname today and scored an NCAA record seven touchdowns in Mississippi's 49–7 rout of Mississippi State.

Boykin, a fullback from Greenville, Miss., ran out of the middle spot in the Rebels' split "T" formation when quarterback Jimmy Lear wasn't calling pass plays. Boykin scored on runs of 14, 12, 17, 13, 85, 1, and 5 yards, while Lear kicked all the extra points.

In addition to the victory, the Rebels will take the "Golden Egg" back with them to Oxford for the fifth straight year. The mounted gold football is symbolic of victory in this 50-year-old intra-state battle.

Most touchdowns scored, major college game: 7, Arnold "Showboat" Boykin, Mississippi, vs. Mississippi State, Dec. 1, 1951

Jim Brown's Greatest Act

SYRACUSE, N.Y., Nov. 17, 1956—Archbold Stadium was sold out today as more than 40,000 people were on hand to see Jimmy Brown in his last regular-season game as a collegian. The All-American running back, who was born on a Georgia sea island and grew up on New York's Long Island, didn't disappoint Syracuse fans as he put on one of the greatest one-man shows in major college history.

Brown broke loose for six touchdowns and kicked seven extra points in scoring a total of 43 points in Syracuse's 61–7 romp over Colgate. The soft-spoken Brown picked up 197 yards rushing on 22 carries and scored on runs of 15, 50, 8, and 19 yards as well as a pair of plunges from inside the 1-yard line. In totally dominating the game, the Orangemen picked up

Syracuse's Jimmy Brown scored 43 points in a game against Colgate.

UPI

511 yards rushing, never had to punt, and intercepted five Colgate passes.

Most points, major college game: 43, Jimmy Brown, Syracuse, vs. Colgate, Nov. 17, 1956 (six touchdowns, seven PATs)

Rhome Not Built in a Day

TULSA, Okla., Nov. 26, 1964—Tulsa quarterback Jerry Rhome was in there throwing today, completing 18 of 29 passes for 234 yards and two touchdowns as he concluded a record-breaking collegiate career while leading the Hurricanes past Wichita, 21–7.

During the season, the Dallas native was successful on 224 of 326 passes, an average of 68.7 percent. In addition, Rhome threw 198 consecutive passes without an interception, another record. That streak, which started Oct. 17 against Louisville, ended today, not by an interception but by the end of the season.

Among Rhome's achievements are the most touchdowns responsible for in a game, when he passed for seven and ran for two against Louisville; most points responsible for, in that same game, with nine touchdowns and a two-point conversion; and the highest percentage of passes completed in a college career, 448 out of 713, for 62.8 percent.

Even though Wichita didn't win today's game, the Shockers did manage to halt Rhome 26 yards short of the career record for total offense. And Howard Twilley, Rhome's favorite receiver and the leading pass-catcher in the country—who grabbed 10 tosses for 139 yards today—came up two points shy of the national scoring championship. Twilley, who usually kicks extra points, got one record this season when he scored six two-point conversions on pass receptions. This ties the mark for two-point conversions for a season and established a seasonal mark for two-pointers on passes.

Most consecutive passes without an interception: 198, Jerry Rhome, Tulsa, October 17–November 26, 1964
Most points responsible for, game: 56, Jerry Rhome, Tulsa, vs. Louisville, October 17, 1964 (seven touchdowns passed for, two touchdowns scored, one two-point conversion passed for)

Beware the Hurricane

TULSA, Okla., Nov. 25, 1965—Bill Anderson uncorked fourth-quarter scoring passes of 60, 63, 51, and 13 yards to give the Tulsa Hurricane a come-from-behind victory today over Colorado State University, 48–20. In addition, Howard Twilley caught two TD passes and kicked four extra points to give him 127 points as he became the first receiver ever to win a national scoring title.

Anderson, who had thrown only one varsity pass (incomplete) before this season while backing up Jerry Rhome, finished the year with a whole batch of records following today's 37 completions in 57 attempts for 502 yards and five touchdowns. Twilley, runner-up to Southern California's Mike Garrett in the Heisman Trophy balloting this year, caught 19 passes for 214 yards today. The 19 receptions were one more than his previous single-game record.

Between them, Anderson and Twilley finished with these NCAA major college records:

Most passes attempted, season: 509, Bill Anderson, Tulsa, 1965

Most passes attempted per game, season: 50.9, Bill Anderson, Tulsa, 1965

Most passes completed per game, season: 29.6, Bill Anderson, Tulsa, 1965

Most plays, per game, season: 58.0, Bill Anderson, Tulsa, 1965

Most passes caught, season: 134, Howard Twilley, Tulsa, 1965

Most passes caught, career: 261, Howard Twilley, Tulsa, 1963–65

Most passes caught per game, season: 13.4, Howard Twilley, Tulsa, 1965

Most passes caught per game, career: 10.0, Howard Twilley, Tulsa, 1963–65

Most yards gained, pass receptions, season: 1,779, Howard Twilley, Tulsa, 1965

Most yards gained, pass receptions, per game, season: 177.9, Howard Twilley, Tulsa, 1965

Highest average gain on pass receptions, career: 128.6 yards per game, Howard Twilley, Tulsa, 1963–65

Virgil's Standard

PROVO, Utah, Nov. 5, 1966—Brigham Young's Virgil Carter thrilled a homecoming crowd of 30,184 today as his record-breaking passing performance carried the Cougars to a 53–33 triumph over Texas Western.

Brigham Young's Virgil Carter totaled 599 yards rushing and passing in one game.

The slender senior, who majors in statistics, made good on 29 of 47 passing attempts for five touchdowns and 513 yards. In addition, Carter scrambled for 86 yards, giving him a combined total of 599 yards, an NCAA total offense record for one game.

While Carter, who received a standing ovation when he left the game with four minutes left to play, was working his aerial magic, his counterpart at Texas Western was gamely trying to keep the Miners in the game. Billy Stevens, one of the leading passers in the nation the last two seasons, completed 22 of 47 attempts but was hurt by three interceptions and a pair of fumbles.

Most total yardage, running and passing: 599 yards, Virgil Carter, Brigham Young, vs. Texas Western, Nov. 5, 1966

Pruitt Can Do It

STILLWATER, Okla., Dec. 4, 1971—Oklahoma's wishbone, which broke against Nebraska on Thanksgiving Day, was working like magic today as the booming Sooners rolled over Oklahoma State, 58–14.

With Jack Mildren pitching and Greg Pruitt running, the wishbone "T" formation enabled Oklahoma to amass 584 yards on 69 rushing plays. Pruitt, who scored twice, picked up 189 yards and had sprints of 29, 32, and 64 yards. The junior from Houston, Tex., finished the season with 1,665 yards in 178 carries for an NCAA record average of 9.35 yards per attempt.

Mildren, the kind of running quarterback needed to make a wishbone attack effective, also scored two touchdowns in leading Oklahoma to its tenth victory in 11 games. The lone defeat came at the hands of top-ranked Nebraska on Thanksgiving Day.

Highest rushing average, season (minimum 150 attempts): 9.35 yards per carry (178 rushes for 1,665 yards), Greg Pruitt, Oklahoma, 1971

'Husker Hustler

LINCOLN, Neb., Nov. 18, 1972—Nebraska's Johnny Rodgers opened the scoring today with a 52-yard runback of a Kansas State punt for a touchdown and the Cornhuskers didn't stop scoring until they had whipped Kansas State, 59–7. The victory was the 100th in coach Bob Devaney's 11 years at Nebraska.

Rodgers also scored a touchdown in the second quarter, on an 8-yard run, before the game was turned over to the reserves. The touchdown on the punt return gave Rodgers a pair of NCAA records. It was the seventh time he had run back a punt for a TD, tying him with Oklahoma's Jack Mitchell in that department. Rodgers had also run back a kickoff for a touchdown, matching the eight TDs on kick returns by Colorado's Cliff Branch.

Most touchdowns on kick returns, career: 8, Johnny Rodgers, Nebraska, 1970–72 (seven punts, one kickoff) (Ties Cliff Branch, Colorado, 1970–71 [six punts, two kickoffs])
Most touchdowns on punt returns, major college career: 7, Johnny Rodgers, Nebraska, 1970–72 (Ties Jack Mitchell, Oklahoma, 1946–48)

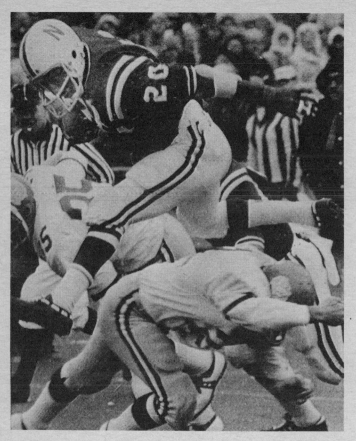

In this game against Kansas State, Nebraska's Johnny Rodgers tied two kick-return marks. *UPI*

Panther on the Prowl

PITTSBURGH, Pa., Nov. 26, 1976—Tony Dorsett, the No. 1 running back in the country, carried the ball for 224 yards and two touchdowns tonight in leading the No. 1-ranked Pitt Panthers to a 24–7 victory over Penn State.

Pittsburgh's Tony Dorsett, scoring here against Notre Dame, made a number of marks in his four-year career.   *UPI*

Establishing several NCAA records with his efforts on the wet and slippery artificial turf before a crowd of 50,360 in Three Rivers Stadium, Dorsett helped Pitt complete its first unbeaten season since 1937, when the Panthers were also the top-ranked college football team.

The 5-foot 11-inch Dorsett, son of an Aliquippa, Pa., steel mill worker, became the first collegian to pass the 6,000-yard mark in rushing, as his 224 yards gave him a four-year total of 6,082. He finished the night with 28 school records plus 11 NCAA records and a share of three others, some of which seem destined to stand for a long time.

Most yards gained rushing, career: 6,082, Tony Dorsett, Pittsburgh, 1973–76
Most rushes, career: 1,074, Tony Dorsett, Pittsburgh, 1973–76

Most games gaining 100 yards or more: 33, Tony Dorsett, Pittsburgh,
1973–76 (Ties Archie Griffin, Ohio State, 1972–75)
Most touchdowns, career: 59, Tony Dorsett, Pittsburgh, 1973–76 (Ties
Glenn Davis, Army, 1943–46)
Most games scoring two or more touchdowns, career: 17, Tony Dorsett,
Pittsburgh, 1973–76 (Ties Steve Owens, Oklahoma, 1967–69, and
Glenn Davis, Army, 1943–46)
Most consecutive games scoring two or more touchdowns: 7, Tony
Dorsett, Pittsburgh, 1976

Ivery Coasts

AIR FORCE ACADEMY, Colo., Nov. 11, 1978—Georgia
Tech's senior tailback Eddie Lee Ivery scored today on touchdown runs of 73, 80, and 57 yards in amassing 356 yards rushing
as the Ramblin' Wreck overwhelmed the Air Force Academy,
42–21.

Carrying the ball 26 times in bitter cold weather, a light
snowfall, and constant fog, the 6-foot, 200-pound Ivery opened
the fourth quarter with his 57-yard touchdown jaunt to break
the spirit of the scrambling Falcons, who had pulled within
seven points of the Engineers.

Ivery, a native of McDuffie, Ga., eclipsed the NCAA single-
game rushing mark of 350 yards set by Michigan State's Eric
Allen against Purdue in 1971.

Highest rushing average, game (minimum 25 rushes): 13.7 yards per
carry, Eddie Lee Ivery, Georgia Tech, Nov. 11, 1978

Sooner Boomer

NORMAN, Okla., Nov. 18, 1978—Heisman Trophy candidate
Billy Sims was the big news today, scoring on touchdown runs
of 1, 35, 2, and 9 yards as Oklahoma routed cross-state rival
Oklahoma State, 62–7.

It was German-born placekicker Uwe von Schamann, though,
whose name entered the record book as he connected on all
eight point-after-touchdown attempts to complete a perfect season of 59 extra points in 59 tries.

Born Uwe Detlef Walter von Schamann in West Berlin, the
kicker moved with his mother to Fort Worth, Tex., as a young
man before enrolling at Oklahoma. As a kicker for the Sooners

for three seasons, he clicked on 140 of 141 extra-point attempts, including 125 in a row starting with the Oklahoma-Oklahoma State game two years ago.

Best perfect record of extra points made, season: 59 of 59, Uwe von Schamann, Oklahoma, 1978

Most consecutive extra points, season: 59, Uwe von Schamann, Oklahoma, 1978

Most consecutive extra points, career: 125, Uwe von Schamann, Oklahoma (started October 23, 1976, vs. Oklahoma State; last 19 in 1976, all 47 in 1977, all 59 in 1978)

Highest percentage of extra points made, career (minimum 100 attempts): 99.3 percent, Uwe von Schamann, Oklahoma, 1976–78 (140 of 141)

McMahon Aloft

PROVO, Utah, Nov. 21, 1981—Brigham Young quarterback Jim McMahon completed 35 of 54 passes for 565 yards and four touchdowns today as the Cougars romped over the University of Utah, 56–28.

Brigham Young's Jim McMahon rewrote many collegiate passing records.

UPI

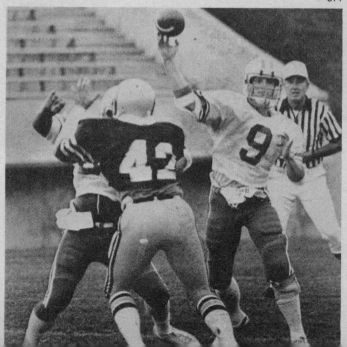

With the Western Athletic Conference title and a Holiday Bowl bid waiting for the winner of this traditional intra-state clash, Utah jumped off to an early 10–7 lead before McMahon threw an 8-yard scoring strike to Gordon Hudson to give BYU a lead it never relinquished. The 6-foot 1-inch, 180-pound McMahon also hit on touchdown passes of 6, 27, and 37 yards in front of a record crowd of 47,163.

McMahon, who was born in Jersey City, N.J., and grew up in California, ended his final regular-season game owning or sharing 57 NCAA records. Among the marks are total offense standards for three years and having had a hand in more touchdowns and more points than anyone else.

Most yards gained, three seasons: 9,640, Jim McMahon, Brigham Young, 1978, 1980–81 (9,433 passing, 207 rushing)

Most yards gained, season: 4,627, Jim McMahon, Brigham Young, 1980 (4,571 passing, 56 rushing)

Most yards gained, two seasons, 8,085, Jim McMahon, Brigham Young, 1980–81 (8,126 passing, minus 41 rushing)

Most yards gained per game: 367.5, Jim McMahon, Brigham Young, 1980–81 (8,085 in 22 games)

Most touchdowns responsible for, career: 94, Jim McMahon, Brigham Young, 1977–78, 1980–81 (scored 10, passed for 84)

Most points responsible for, career: 568, Jim McMahon, Brigham Young, 1977–78, 1980–81 (scored 10 TDs, passed for 84 TDs, accounted for two two-point conversions)

Young and Accurate

PROVO, Utah, Nov. 19, 1983—Steve Young, a direct descendant of Brigham Young, closed out his college career here today by throwing six touchdown passes as Brigham Young University routed the University of Utah, 55–7.

Passing with remarkable accuracy, the lefthanded Young connected on 22 of 25 passes for 268 yards, giving him a completion average for the season of 71.3 percent as he clicked on 306 passes in 429 attempts.

Utilizing five different receivers on his scoring throws, the 6-foot 2-inch Young also extended his string of games in which he has thrown at least one touchdown pass to 22, dating back to last year's season opener.

Highest percentage of passes completed, season: 71.3 percent, Steve Young, Brigham Young, 1983 (306 of 429)

Most consecutive games throwing a touchdown pass: 22, Steve Young,
Brigham Young, Sept. 2, 1982, through 1983
Highest average gain per play, minimum 6,500 yards: 7.49, Steve Young,
Brigham Young, 1981–83 (1,177 for 8,817 yards)
Most games gaining 300 yards or more, career: 18, Steve Young, Brig-
ham Young, 1981–83
Most yards gained per game, season: 395.1, Steve Young, Brigham
Young, 1983

Rozier's Harvest

NORMAN, Okla., Nov. 26, 1983—Mike Rozier helped Nebraska gain an Orange Bowl berth and strengthened his own
Heisman Trophy bid as he carried the ball 32 times for 205
yards and scored a touchdown in the Cornhuskers' 28–21 victory over archrival Oklahoma.

Before 75,008 fans at Owen Field, the 5-foot 10-inch, 198-
pound Rozier, a native of Camden, N.J., tied the score at
14–14 on a 3-yard run late in the first half. Then in the third
quarter, on the first play from scrimmage after the Sooners
had gone up 21–14, Rozier took off on a 62-yard jaunt to the
three-yard line to set up another tying touchdown en route to
the Nebraska victory.

Rozier's touchdown was his 29th of the season, trying the
NCAA mark established by Penn State's Lydell Mitchell in
1971.

Most touchdowns rushing, season: 29, Mike Rozier, Nebraska, 1983
(Ties Lydell Mitchell, Penn State, 1971)
Most points scored, season: 174, Mike Rozier, Nebraska, 1983 (Ties
Lydell Mitchell, Penn State, 1971)
Highest average gain per rush, career (minimum 500 carries): 7.16, Mike
Rozier, Nebraska, 1981–83 (668 for 4,780)

A-mayesing

EUGENE, Ore., Oct. 27, 1984—Junior running back Rueben
Mayes established an NCAA single-game rushing record today,
gaining 357 yards on 39 carries as he led the Washington State
Cougars to a 50–41 victory over Pac-10 rival Oregon.

The 5-foot 11-inch, 198-pound Mayes, a native of North
Battleford, Sask., Canada, scored on runs of 2, 69, and 12
yards. He rolled for 197 yards in the first half and then, with

Nebraska's Mike Rozier owns the highest-gain-per-rush record. *UPI*

just one minute and 12 seconds left to play in the game, he squeezed out his last four yards of the day. That was enough to put him one yard over the 356 yards gained by Georgia Tech's Eddie Lee Ivery against the Air Force Academy in 1978.

Most yards gained, game: Rueben Mayes, Washington State, vs. Oregon, Oct. 27, 1984

Flutie Flips

MIAMI, Fla., Nov. 23, 1984—An unbelievable pass by Doug Flutie and an incredible reception by Gerard Phelan gave Boston College an improbable 47–45 victory over the University of Miami after time had run out in the Orange Bowl here today.

With six seconds showing on the clock and the Hurricanes of Miami leading, 45–41, Boston College lined up at the Miami 48-yard line. Flutie had called the "flood tip" play in which he intended to throw the ball to his roommate, wide receiver Phelan, who in turn would try to tip the ball to one of two other receivers flooding the zone.

Instead, after circling back to his own 37-yard line to avoid the Miami rush, the 5-foot 10-inch Flutie uncorked a 64-yard throw to Phelan, waiting one yard deep in the end zone as three Hurricane defenders fell over themselves in front of him. With no one to tip the ball to, Phelan held onto it for the score.

The pass was Flutie's 34th completion in 46 attempts, good for 472 yards, as he outdueled Miami's sophomore sensation Bernie Kosar, who went 25 of 38 for 447 yards as he kept the Hurricanes in the seesaw game. Flutie also rushed for 45 yards, enabling him to become the first collegian to surpass 10,000 yards in total offense.

Most net yards gained running and passing by two players: 953, Doug Flutie (517), Boston College, and Bernie Kosar (436), Miami (Fla.), Nov. 23, 1984

Big Man on Little Campus

PLYMOUTH, N.H., Nov. 9, 1985—Playing in his final college game, Plymouth State running back Joe Dudek established three all-division NCAA scoring records today as he accounted for four touchdowns in the Panthers' 43–7 romp over the Curry College Colonels of Milton, Mass.

Playing at the Division III level, where there are no athletic scholarships, the 6-foot-1, 195-pound Dudek, a native of Quincy, Mass., finished his career with 474 points on 79 TDs, all but three of them rushing. The 125 yards he gained on the ground today pushed his four-year total to 5,570 yards and a 7.1-yard average.

Dudek's five touchdowns two weeks ago against Bridgewater

Boston College's Doug Flutie was the first collegian to achieve 10,000 yards in total offense. *Boston College*

(Mass.) State put him past the NCAA record of 66 set by Walter Payton at Jackson State and the NAIA record of 70 established by Wilbert Montgomery when he was playing at Abilene Christian.

Most touchdowns scored by rushing, career: 76, Joe Dudek, Plymouth State, 1982–85
Most touchdowns, career: 79, Joe Dudek, Plymouth State, 1982–85
Most points, career: 474, Joe Dudek, Plymouth State, 1982–85

Joe Dudek of Plymouth State broke Walter Payton's NCAA mark for most rushing touchdowns.
Plymouth State

COLLEGE BASKETBALL

Backboard Dukes

NEW YORK, March 14, 1953—No. 1-seeded Seton Hall had little trouble with St. John's University tonight as 7-foot Walter Dukes led the Pirates to a 58–46 victory and the National Invitation Tournament championship before a crowd of 18,496, the largest ever to watch a collegiate game in Madison Square Garden.

Dukes, the first black to win unanimous All-American honors, scored 21 points and pulled down 20 rebounds en route to winning the tournament MVP trophy. The 20 rebounds brought his total for the season to 734, an all-time record. Dukes is a native of Rochester, N.Y., where he was spotted working in his mother's dry cleaning store by Bob Davies of the Rochester Royals, a former Seton Hall star. Davies persuaded Dukes to attend Seton Hall, located in South Orange, N.J.

Tonight's championship was accomplished with the same ease that the Pirates displayed in compiling a 28–2 regular-

Seton Hall's Walter Dukes receives the MVP award for his play in the NIT.   *UPI*

season record before sweeping Niagara, Manhattan, and St. John's in the NIT. Little Richie Regan was the floor leader, racking up seven assists on feeds to Dukes and scoring 13 points.

Most rebounds, major college season: 734, Walter Dukes, Seton Hall, 1952–53

Paladin's Gun

GREENVILLE, S.C., Feb. 13, 1954—Paladin Frank Selvy used his gun often and well tonight as he shot the basketball through the hoop for a record 100 points in leading Furman to a 149–95 rout of little Newberry College.

The 6-foot 3-inch Selvy put on the show for his parents, who were visiting with a few friends from his hometown of Corbin, Ky. The Furman senior, the leading scorer in the nation, started out with 24 points in the first quarter and added another 13 in the second. By the end of the third period, he had 62 and his teammates began to feed him the ball every time the Paladins were on offense.

By the middle of the fourth quarter he had broken the NCAA record of 73 points in one game, set by Temple's Bill Mlkvy in 1951. Selvy was also lucky that Newberry didn't try to stall or slow the game down in order to frustrate his shooting for the record. By the time the final gun sounded, Selvy had pumped in 38 points in the period to give him a nice round figure—100 points.

Most points, major college game: 100, Frank Selvy, Furman, vs. Newberry, Feb. 13, 1954

Tar Heel String

KANSAS CITY, Mo., March 23, 1957—For the second time in two nights, North Carolina was forced into triple overtime before emerging victorious as the Tar Heels defeated Kansas, 54–53, and won the NCAA basketball championship. The triumph was the 32nd straight this season for North Carolina, a collegiate record for most victories in an undefeated season.

In the semifinal game last night, Lennie Rosenbluth hit two quick jump shots to lift the Tar Heels past Michigan State, 74–

Furman's Frank Selvy scored 100 points in a college game. *UPI*

70, in triple-overtime. Tonight, it was Joe Quigg's two free throws in the last six seconds of the third extra period that provided the one-point margin of victory. Even after Quigg had made good on the foul shots, he had to block a pass intended for Kansas' 7-foot center, Wilt Chamberlain, to preserve the victory.

Most victories, undefeated season: 32, North Carolina, 1956–57

Carr's Finer Points

DAYTON, Ohio, March 7, 1970—Hitting from long range as well as on driving layups, Austin Carr scored a record 61 points tonight in leading Notre Dame to a 112–82 rout of Ohio University in the opening round of the NCAA Mideast Regional basketball tournament.

The 6-foot 3-inch Carr, a product of Mackin High School in Washington, D.C., broke the tournament record of 58 points set by Princeton's Bill Bradley in 1965. Carr hit on 25 of 44 field goal attempts and 11 of 14 foul shots for his 61 points.

Most points, NCAA tournament, game: 61, Austin Carr, Notre Dame, vs. Ohio University, March 7, 1970

Notre Dame's Austin Carr scored 61 points against Ohio U.　　*UPI*

The Pistol's Parting Shots

NEW YORK, March 19, 1970—"Pistol Pete" Maravich, the highest scorer in major college history, was held to 20 points in the final game of his college career tonight as Marquette whipped Louisiana State, 101–79, to advance to the finals of the National Invitation Tournament at Madison Square Garden.

Maravich was hampered by an ankle injury sustained in a quarterfinal-round victory over Oklahoma in which he pumped in 37 points. Tonight, not only did the Warriors double-team him, but they also choked off the passing lanes so Maravich could not feed his teammates with passes that are often as dazzling and unorthodox as his shots. The ankle injury will keep Pete out of tomorrow afternoon's consolation game against Jacksonville.

Maravich, who has played his entire varsity career under the coaching of his father, Press, thus finished with these collegiate records:

Most points, major college, season: 1,381, Pete Maravich, LSU, 1969–70
Highest scoring average, major college, season: 44.5 points per game, Pete Maravich, LSU, 1969–70
Most field goals attempted, major college, season: 1,168, Pete Maravich, LSU, 1969–70
Most field goals made, major college, season: 522, Pete Maravich, LSU, 1969–70
Most points, major college, career: 3,667, Pete Maravich, LSU, 1967 68 to 1969–70
Highest scoring average, major college, career: 44.2 points per game, Pete Maravich, LSU, 1967–68 to 1969–70
Most field goals made, major college, career: 1,387, Pete Maravich, LSU, 1967–68 to 1969–70

Bruin Power

SOUTH BEND, Ind., Jan. 19, 1974—A short jump shot by Dwight Clay with 29 seconds left to play provided a one-point victory for Notre Dame today, 71–70, as the Fighting Irish snapped UCLA's winning streak at 88, the longest in college basketball history. The Uclans had made Iowa their 88th consecutive victim in a game two nights ago at the Chicago Stadium, winning easily, 68–44.

Prolific "Pistol Pete" Maravich of LSU ended his collegiate career in the NIT. *UPI*

Notre Dame's Dwight Clay led the upset that ended UCLA's 88-game winning streak.

UPI

The last time the Bruins had lost a game was on this same court three years ago—Jan. 23, 1971—when Austin Carr's 46 points led Notre Dame to victory. Since that time, UCLA won its fifth, sixth, and seventh consecutive NCAA championships.

UCLA's record streak started Jan. 30, 1971, with a 74–61 victory over the University of California at Santa Barbara. The Bruins depended then on players like Curtis Rowe, Sidney Wicks, Steve Patterson, and Henry Bibby. The next three years the mainstays were Bill Walton and Keith Wilkes. Today was the first time in their varsity careers that Walton and Wilkes were on the losing side.

The game between UCLA and Notre Dame was billed as a showdown between the teams' two centers, 6-foot 11-inch Walton and 6-foot 9-inch John Shumate of ND. Each scored 24 points, rebounded well, and played tough defense. The difference was the ball-handling and shooting of Notre Dame's 6-foot 4-inch Gary Brokaw, who scored 25 points, led a burst in the last three minutes in which the Irish outscored UCLA 12–0, and found Clay open for the final score of the game.

Most consecutive victories: 88, UCLA, Jan. 30, 1971, to Jan. 17, 1974

Runnin' (and Shootin') Rebels

HONOLULU, Hawaii, Feb. 21, 1976—Playing against a University of Hawaii squad with just eight members in uniform, the University of Nevada–Las Vegas tonight played its usual run-and-gun style of basketball as the Runnin' Rebels rolled to a 114–99 victory.

Sixth-ranked and now sporting a 26–1 record, the Rebels finished their regular-season schedule with a scoring average of 110.5 points a game, the highest in NCAA history. Shooting a torrid 66.7 percent from the field, UNLV was led by native Las Vegan Sam Smith with 32 points, followed by Lewis Brown, 20; Jackie Robinson, 19; Eddie Owen, 16; and Glen Gondrezick, 12.

During the season UNLV, which lost only to Pepperdine along the way, got a considerable boost in its scoring average when it defeated little Hawaii-Hilo by scoring 164 points, which also put the Rebels in the scoring book for most points scored by one team in a game.

Highest team scoring average, regular season: 110.5 points per game, Nevada–Las Vegas, 1975–76

Most points scored by one team, game: 164, Nevada–Las Vegas, vs. Hawaii-Hilo, Feb. 19, 1976

Herculean Heave

HUNTINGTON, W.Va., Feb. 7, 1985—Desperation shots at the end of a half or game are commonplace in basketball, but Bruce Morris of Marshall University did the uncommon tonight. He sank a shot from 92 feet, 5¼ inches away from the basket.

Bruce Morris of Marshall University sank the longest shot.   *Marshall*

With just three seconds remaining in the first half of a game against Appalachian State, the 6-foot 4-inch Morris picked up a blocked shot at the baseline. He turned and, heaving the ball like a baseball, sent it swishing through the net at the other end of the court. Marshall went on to win the game, 93–82.

Morris, a native of Deerfield, Ill., described how it happened afterward. "The ball just fell straight down in my arms, and I turned and saw the clock and just let it go. When I saw it going, I knew it would hit something or be pretty close because it looked kind of accurate."

As the low-trajectory shot slipped through the hoop, he said, "I looked at the ref to see if it had counted, and it did."

Longest field goal: 92 feet, 5¼ inches, Bruce Morris, Marshall, vs. Appalachian State, Feb. 7, 1985

TRACK AND FIELD

To the End of the Pit

MEXICO CITY, Mexico, Oct. 18, 1968—Long jumper Bob Beamon was about to make his first jump in the Olympic Games. He pounded down the runway, hit the takeoff board in full stride, and as soon as he lifted off the ground, he flapped his arms as though he would gain greater height through flight. When Beamon landed at the far end of the pit today in Olympic Stadium, he was 29 feet, 2½ inches away from where he had started.

The 22-year-old Beamon, a native of Jamaica, Queens, in New York City, had broken the world record in the long jump by nearly two feet. The old mark of 27 feet, 4¾ inches was shared by Ralph Boston of the United States and Igor Ter-Ovanesyan of the Soviet Union.

World record, long jump: 29 feet, 2½ inches, Bob Beamon, Oct. 18, 1968

Victory as Protest

MEXICO CITY, Mexico, Oct., 18, 1968—Wearing black socks in silent protest over the treatment of other American black athletes, Lee Evans raced to a world record of 43.8 seconds in winning the 400-meter dash today at the Olympic Games. Evans was followed across the finish line by Larry James and Ron Freeman, both American and both black, as the United States swept the event.

Evans wore the black socks to protest the dismissal of Tommie Smith and John Carlos from the U.S. squad after they gave a blackpower salute on the victory stand following their first- and third-place finishes in the 200-meter dash. Evans' time of 43.8 seconds today was seven-tenths of a second better than the listed world record.

World record, 400 meters: 43.8, Lee Evans, Oct. 18, 1968

Four for the Record

MEXICO CITY, Mexico, Oct. 20, 1968—Lee Evans of San Jose, Cal., Larry James of White Plains, N.Y., and Ron

Bob Beamon shatters the world record in the long jump at the Olympics in Mexico City. *UPI*

Freeman of Elizabeth, N.J., who finished one-two-three in the 400-meter run two days ago, were joined by Vince Matthews of Brooklyn, N.Y., today and the United States runners raced to a world record in winning the Olympic gold medal in the 1,600-meter relay.

Matthews opened up with a 45-second leg, while the others with running starts were caught in splits of 43.2 seconds for Freeman, 43.8 seconds for James, and 44.1 seconds for Evans. Their time of 2 minutes, 56.1 seconds, bettered the old mark by 3.5 seconds.

World record, 4 × 400-meter relay: 2:56.1, United States national team (Vince Matthews, Ron Freeman, Larry James, and Lee Evans), Oct. 20, 1968

Lee Evans posts a record 43.8 in the Olympic 100-meter run in Mexico City.   *UPI*

Record-breaking U.S. 1600-meter relay team of Lee Evans, Ron Freeman (partially hidden), Larry James, and Vince Matthews gives the black-power salute on victors' stand in Mexico City.   *UPI*

California Gold Rush

LOS ANGELES, Cal., Aug. 11, 1984—Running the anchor leg of the 4 × 100-meter relay, Carl Lewis took the baton with a three-meter lead and stretched it into a seven-meter margin at the finish line as he earned his fourth gold medal of the Olympic Games today.

The 23-year-old Lewis had already won gold medals by taking the 100-meter dash in 9.99 seconds, the 200 meters in

Olympic record time of 19.80 seconds, and the long jump with a leap of 8.54 meters, or 28 feet, ¼ inch. The relay quartet of Sam Graddy, Ron Brown, Calvin Smith, and Lewis produced the only track-and-field world record of the Los Angeles Olympics, with a time of 37.83 seconds.

Lewis's four track-and-field gold medals matched the achievement of Jesse Owens, who earned them in the same four events as Lewis, in the 1936 Games held in Berlin.

Born in Birmingham, Ala., raised in Willingboro, N.J., and currently a resident of Houston, Tex., where he attended the University of Houston, Lewis recalled the one time he had met Owens. "Jesse Owens is still the same to me—a legend," Lewis said after winning his fourth medal. "Without the inspiration he gave me, I wouldn't be here today."

Most gold medals won, track and field, one Olympics: 4, Carl Lewis, Los Angeles, 1984 (Ties Jesse Owens, U.S., Berlin, 1936)

Carl Lewis nears the finish in the 200-meter run, one of his four gold-medal events at the Olympics in Los Angeles.   *Wide World*

GOLF

"The Haig"

DALLAS, Texas, Nov. 5, 1927—Walter Hagen rallied from three holes behind today to defeat Joe Turnesa, one up, and win his fourth consecutive Professional Golfers Association championship. It was the fifth time the dark-eyed, slick-haired Hagen, known as "The Haig," has won the event.

Turnesa did not give up easily, going one up on the first nine holes this morning, picking up another on the back nine, and

Walter Hagen won the most consecutive PGA championships.   *UPI*

going three up on the first hole of the afternoon round. Hagen, a native of Rochester, N.Y., came on strong after that, however, and pecked away at the lead until he went one up on the 13th hole. The two men played even the rest of the way.

Hagen won his first PGA in 1921. Two years later he was beaten by Gene Sarazen in a memorable contest at the Pelham Country Club in New York. Since then, The Haig has won them all, a record four in a row.

Most consecutive PGA championships: 4, Walter Hagen, 1924–27

Link to Greatness

ARDMORE, Pa., Sept. 27, 1930—The crowd around the 11th green at the Merion Cricket Club hushed as Bobby Jones addressed the ball. Jones—trying to become the only man ever to complete a golfing "grand slam"—stood about 20 feet from the cup. He tapped the ball gently. It rolled toward the cup, but slowed too quickly. It did not have the legs.

The 28-year-old Southern gentleman from Atlanta was not really trying to make the putt, though. He wanted a good shot, but more importantly, he wanted to put the pressure on his championship-round opponent, Gene Homans.

In May, Jones had won the British Amateur title at St. Andrews; in June he took the British Open at Hoylake and the U.S. Open at Interlachen, near Minneapolis. Now the U.S. Amateur was at stake. Jones had led all scorers in the 36-hole qualifying round of medal play and had breezed through the opening rounds of match play in the tourney. In today's 36-hole championship round, on the 29th hole, Jones was eight strokes ahead of Homans with eight holes left to play.

The approach putt by Jones had set up a do-or-die situation for Homans. Both men reached the green in two strokes. Jones's putt was his third shot. Homans had to sink a difficult putt or lose, 8 and 7. Homans' shot never got close. Before the ball had stopped rolling, Homans was crossing the green to shake the hand of the only man ever to complete a golfing grand slam.

Most golf grand slams: 1, Robert Tyre Jones, Jr., 1930

Bobby Jones completes golf's only grand slam in the U.S. Amateur championship at Ardmore, Pa., in 1930.   *UPI*

Queen of Swing

HOPKINS, Minn., Aug. 31, 1935—The galleries were all rooting for 17-year-old local favorite Patty Berg, but Glenna Collett Vare would not be denied today as she won her sixth women's national amateur golf championship on the Interlachen Country Club course here in this Minneapolis suburb.

Berg, a native of Minneapolis who started playing golf only four years ago, went down to defeat as Vare finished with two birdies to go up three holes with two left to play in the 36-hole final round of match play.

Glenna Collett Vare won six national amateur championships. *UPI*

For Vare, it was the latest in a collection of national titles that began in 1922. She won again in 1925 and then three straight years, 1928 to 1930.

Most U.S. national amateur championships: 6, Glenna Collett Vare, Philadelphia, Pennsylvania, 1922, 1925, 1928–30, 1935

Wright On

CHULA VISTA, Cal., July 12, 1964—Mickey Wright sank a seven-foot birdie putt on the 16th hole to take over the lead and hold on for a playoff victory in the United States Women's open golf tournament here today.

Wright and Ruth Jessen were tied at 290 yesterday after 72 holes on the 6,400-yard San Diego Country Club course. Today's birdie putt on the 16th enabled Wright to finish with 70, two strokes better than Jessen in the 18-hole playoff.

The victory for the 29-year-old Wright—her fourth in the U.S. Open—brought her first-prize money of $2,200. Wright is the second woman to win four Opens, the first being Betsy Rawls in 1951, 1953, 1957, and 1960.

Most U.S. women's open golf championships: 4, Mickey Wright, 1958–59, 1961, 1964 (Ties Betsy Rawls, 1951, 1953, 1957, 1960)

Double Eagle from Taiwan

BIRMINGHAM, Mich., June 13, 1985—Tze-Chung Chen, a 27-year-old golfer from Taiwan who didn't take up the game until he was 17, made history today in the first round of the U.S. Open at the Oakland Hills Country Club.

Taking aim at the second green on his second shot, 255 yards from the pin on the par-5 of 527 yards, he hit it perfect for a double eagle, the first ever recorded in the 84-year history of the Open.

T.C., as he is called, ended up with a 5-under-par 65 that gave him the first-round lead. "I feel great and so surprised," Chen said. "I never did it before."

Most double eagles, U.S. Open: 1, Tze-Chung Chen, June 13, 1985, Birmingham, Mich.

The Golden Bear

AUGUSTA, Ga., April 13, 1986—He was considered past his prime, but 46-year-old Jack Nicklaus won his sixth Masters today with one of the most dramatic finishes in the history of golf.

With a spectacular charge over the last 10 holes (7-under-par 33 from No. 9 through No. 18), Nicklaus ended up with a 9-under 279 and a one-stroke triumph over Greg Norman and Tom Kite. The Golden Bear thus broke his own record of five Masters victories.

Nobody in golf history has won more major tournament titles (20) than Nicklaus. He shares the record for most PGA championships (5) with Walter Hagen, and he shares the record for most U.S. Open championships (4) with Ben Hogan, Bobby Jones, and Willie Anderson. And he holds the record for lowest score in a U.S. Open (272).

Most Masters tournament victories: 6, Jack Nicklaus, 1963, 1965, 1966, 1972, 1975, 1986

Most PGA championships: 5, Jack Nicklaus, 1963, 1971, 1973, 1975, 1980 (Ties Walter Hagen, 1921, 1924–27)

Most. U.S. Open championships: 4, Jack Nicklaus, 1962, 1967, 1972, 1980 (Ties Bobby Jones, 1923, 1926, 1929, 1930; and Willie Anderson, 1901, 1903–5)

Most victories, major tournaments: 20, Jack Nicklaus (6 Masters, 5 PGA, 4 U.S. Open, 3 British Open, 2 U.S. Amateur)

Lowest score, U.S. Open: 272, Jack Nicklaus, 1980

Jack Nicklaus hits out of the rough in the fourth of his six Masters triumphs.   *UPI*

TENNIS

Helen Wills Moody won eight Wimbledon singles titles.   *UPI*

Moody Triumph

WIMBLEDON, England, June 2, 1938—Helen Wills Moody, who was among the first to shed the long-sleeve, ankle-length tennis dress, swept to her eighth Wimbledon singles title today by defeating Helen Hull Jacobs.

The victory, 6–4, 6–0, was assured after the eighth game of the first set when Jacobs reinjured her ankle and was virtually immobile on the court the rest of the match.

In a competition that was less than friendly between these two California residents, Jacobs asked no quarter and Moody gave none. This was the 12th time they had met in a championship showdown.

Moody, who was known as "Little Miss Poker Face" in her

younger days, won her first singles title at Wimbledon in 1927, then three more in a row. Her other championships came in 1932, 1933, and 1935.

Most Wimbledon singles titles: 8, Helen Wills Moody, 1927–30, 1932–33, 1935, 1938

Rod's Slam

NEW YORK, Sept. 8, 1969—Rod Laver beat fellow Australian Tony Roche, 7–9, 6–1, 6–2, 6–2, to win the U.S. Open championship at the West Side Tennis Club in Forest Hills today and became the first man ever to complete two tennis grand slams.

The lefthanded Laver duplicated his feat of 1962 when, as an amateur, he won the singles titles at the Australian, French, Wimbledon, and Forest Hills tournaments. This year the 31-year-old Aussie is a pro and earned $16,000 for the U.S. title alone.

The only other man to win a grand slam was American Don Budge, who achieved the honor as an amateur in 1938.

Most tennis grand slams: 2, Rod Laver, 1962, 1969

Rod Laver makes the get as he downs Tony Roche to win the U.S. Open and complete the second of his grand slams in 1969.   *UPI*

Margaret Smith Court defeats Rosemary Casals in the U.S. Open in 1970 to match Maureen Connolly's grand slam.   *UPI*

Court's Court

NEW YORK, Sept. 13, 1970—Australia's Margaret Smith Court defeated Rosemary Casals today to win the U.S. Open tennis championship at Forest Hills and became only the second woman to complete a tennis grand slam.

The 5-foot 9-inch, 145-pound Court came into the match after having defeated Kerry Melville for the Australian title, Helga Niessen for the French championship, and Billie Jean King for Wimbledon honors. All of those were in straight sets. On the center court of the West Side Tennis Club today, however, Casals pushed Court to three sets before the green-eyed Australian prevailed, 6–2, 2–6, 6–1.

Court's sweep of the four national championships duplicates the feat of American Maureen "Little Mo" Connolly in 1953.

Most tennis grand slams, women: 1, Margaret Smith Court, 1970 (Ties Maureen Connolly, 1953)

Boom Boom at Wimbledon

WIMBLEDON, England, July 7, 1985—Defying tradition and logic that said he was too young to win, 17-year-old Boris Becker of West Germany won the Wimbledon men's singles title today.

Boom Boom, as he is nicknamed for good reason, trounced 27-year-old Kevin Curren of the United States, 6–3, 6–7, 7–6, 6–4, to become the youngest champion in the 109-year history of the event.

His triumph also made him the first unseeded player to win and the first German male Wimbledon champion.

Youngest Wimbledon singles champion, men: 17, Boris Becker, 1985

Boris Becker was only 17 when he won the Wimbledon singles crown in 1985. *Wile World*

Martina's Destiny

WIMBLEDON, England, July 5, 1986—Martina Navratilova had talked about how she had never lost a Wimbledon final and wondered how she should react if she did.

Well, the Czechoslovakian-born tennis star didn't have to contend with that today because she won her fifth consecutive women's singles championship, her seventh overall, defeating Hana Mandlikova, 7–6 (7–1), 6–3.

The 29-year-old Navratilova thus was able to tie Suzanne Lenglen as the only women to win five in a row at Wimbledon.

Most consecutive Wimbledon singles championships, women: 5, Martina Navratilova, 1982–86 (Ties Suzanne Lenglen, 1919–23)

Martina Navratilova captured her fifth consecutive Wimbledon singles championship in 1986.   *Wile World*

HORSE RACING

Trainer Ben Jones, with his sixth Kentucky Derby winner, Hill Gail,
Eddie Arcaro up.   *UPI*

Half-Dozen Roses

LOUISVILLE, Ky., May 3, 1952—"Plain Ben" Jones led a
parade of familiar faces to the winner's circle today after 11–10
favorite Hill Gail won the 78th running of the Kentucky Derby.
The race was televised coast-to-coast for the first time.

This was the sixth time Jones had tightened the girth on a
Derby winner, a record number of victories among trainers. It

was also the fifth time Eddie Arcaro had ridden the winner. And it was the fifth time a Calumet Farm horse had won. Mrs. Warren Wright, widow of the Calumet owner, accepted the trophy.

The race itself was not without its suspense, for Hill Gail—who broke from the inside post position—swerved to the outside shortly after the start. After about a half mile, though, Arcaro got a hold on the horse and kept him in front for the remainder of the mile-and-a-quarter classic to finish two lengths in front of Sub Fleet, owned by Charles T. Fisher's Dixiana Farm.

Jones, the grand old man of Derby Racing, saddled Triple Crown winners Whirlaway in 1941 and Citation in 1948, as well as Lawrin in 1938, Pensive in 1944, and Ponder in 1949.

Most Kentucky Derby winners, trainer: 6, Ben Jones—1938, Lawrin; 1941, Whirlaway; 1944, Pensive; 1948, Citation; 1949, Ponder; and 1952, Hill Gail

Majestic Hartack

LOUISVILLE, Ky., May 3, 1969—Undefeated Majestic Prince out of California and Arts and Letters out of New York helped draw the first 100,000-plus crowd into Churchill Downs for today's Kentucky Derby.

When it was over, President Richard Nixon and 106,332 others had seen Majestic Prince, ridden by Bill Hartack, engage Arts and Letters, ridden by Braulio Baeza, at the quarter pole and race almost as one to the wire, where Majestic Prince earned the decision by a neck.

The victory for Hartack was his fifth in the Derby, matching the record number of triumphs by Eddie Arcaro. At the same time, trainer Johnny Longden, who rode Count Fleet to victory here in 1943, became the first man to have both ridden and saddled a Derby winner.

Most Kentucky Derby winners, jockey: 5, Bill Hartack—1957, Iron Leige; 1960, Venetian Way; 1962, Decidedly; 1964, Northern Dancer; and 1969, Majestic Prince (Ties Eddie Arcaro—1938, Lawrin; 1941, Whirlaway; 1945, Hoop Jr.; 1948, Citation; and 1952, Hill Gail)

Ron Turcotte, aboard Secretariat, becomes the fourth jockey to ride consecutive Kentucky Derby winners. *UPI*

Derby Double

LOUISVILLE, Ky., May, 5, 1973—Canadian trainer Lucien Laurin put Canadian jockey Ron Turcotte aboard American-owned and -bred Secretariat, and the big chestnut colt ran himself into the Churchill Downs winner's circle and Turcotte into the Kentucky Derby record book.

Secretariat, owned by Meadow Stable, as was last year's Derby winner Riva Ridge, completed this ninety-ninth running today in the record time of 1 minute, 59 ⅖ seconds in beating Sigmund Sommer's Sham by two-and-a-half lengths.

Turcotte, who rode Riva Ridge in last year's Run for the Roses, became the fourth rider to bring home two horses first in consecutive Derbys. The others were black jockeys Isaac Murphy in 1890 and 1891, and Jimmy Winkfield, 1901 and 1902, and Bobby Ussery in 1967 and 1968, although Ussery's achievement is tainted by the fact that his 1968 winner, Dancer's Image, was eventually disqualified from first place after several years of legal battles.

Most consecutive Kentucky Derby winners, jockey: 2, Ron Turcotte—1972, Riva Ridge, and 1973, Secretariat (Ties Isaac Murphy—1890, Riley, and 1891, Kingman; Jimmy Winkfield—1901, His Eminence, and 1902, Alan-a-Dale; Bobby Ussery—1967, Proud Clarion, and 1968, Dancer's Image)

Record Ride

LAUREL, Md., Dec. 31, 1974—One year ago today, an 18-year-old boy was in the stands at Laurel Race Course here and watched Sandy Hawley ride a horse to victory for the 515th time in the year 1973. Never in thoroughbred history had any jockey been aboard more than 500 winners in a calendar year, and Hawley established a record that many observers felt would stand for years to come.

Chris McCarron, 18, brought 546 horses home first in 1974.   *UPI*

One of those who agreed was the 18-year-old Chris McCarron, who was willing to "bet anything that Sandy's record will stand for 20 years." McCarron was a qualified observer since his older brother Gregg was a jockey, and he himself worked as a stable hand at the racetrack.

A month after Hawley's 515th, McCarron received his jockey's license and rode his first horse, late in January. On February 9 of this year, young Chris rode the first winner of his life. By Dec. 17, just two weeks ago, McCarron rode Ohmylove to a neck victory, beating a horse ridden by brother Gregg. The trip to the winner's circle was the 516th for young McCarron, breaking the less-than-year-old mark established by Hawley.

Chris is an apprentice rider, receiving an advantage in the weight his horses must carry because of his inexperience. But what he lacks in experience, he makes up in ability. Once he realized the record was within his reach, he began riding seven days a week. He rode here in Maryland Monday through Saturday, and on Sundays traveled to the Penn National course near Harrisburg, Pa. He became only the second rider to surpass the 500 victory mark in one year. Then he broke the all-time record. And in today's seventh race, on the last day of the year, he rode Sarah Percy to victory in the feature race of the day. The mare was a 3–5 favorite, and McCarron made the chalk players happy by bringing her home three and a half lengths in front for his 546th victory of the year.

Most winners, year, jockey: 546, Chris McCarron, 1974

AUTO RACING

A.J. Foyt gets the checkered flag as he wins the Indy 500 for the fourth time in 1977. *Wide World*

Foyt's Fourth 500

INDIANAPOLIS, Ind., May 29, 1977—It took him 10 years of trying, but 42-year-old A. J. Foyt Jr. finally won a record fourth Indianapolis 500 today, taking over on the 185th lap of the 200-lap race when Gordon Johncock's engine blew.

The Texas-born Foyt then cautiously protected his lead, "talking to the good Lord and praying," as he put it afterward, to finish 28 seconds ahead of Tom Sneva.

Foyt, whose initials stand for Anthony Joseph, raced 200 times around the 2.5-mile oval in 3 hours, 5 minutes, and 57.7 seconds for an average speed of 161.331 m.p.h.

Today's race was also marked by the first appearance of a woman driver in the Indy 500. Janet Guthrie, a 39-year-old physicist, airplane pilot, and racing driver, qualified with an average speed of 188.404 m.p.h., but engine problems forced her out of the race after 27 laps. She placed 29th in the field of 33.

Most victories, Indianapolis 500: 4, A. J. Foyt Jr., 1961, 1964, 1967, 1977

Fastest Indy

INDIANAPOLIS, Ind., May 27, 1984—Ray Mears won the fastest Indianapolis 500 in history by nearly two laps today—the widest margin in 17 years—as he averaged 163.612 miles an hour.

It was the second time the 32-year-old Californian has won the race. He finished in front of Roberto Guerrero and Al Unser Sr. after last year's winner Tom Sneva dropped out on the 168th lap. Mears's previous victory came in 1979 in only his second start at the Indianapolis Speedway.

The speed record was not totally unanticipated since this was the fastest field ever to qualify for the race, with the 33 starters averaging 205 miles an hour in trials. No one, however, surpassed Mears's qualifying lap record of 208.7 m.p.h. set two years ago.

In today's going, speed records were set on the first 50 laps until the yellow caution flag came out on the 50th lap and the race developed into a tactical duel between Mears and Sneva.

Fastest average time, Indianapolis 500: 163.612 m.p.h., Ray Mears, May 27, 1984

SWIMMING

Mark Spitz butterflies his way to a seventh Olympic gold medal.   *UPI*

Spitz's Spritz

MUNICH, West Germany, Sept. 4, 1972—Mark Spitz picked up his seventh Olympic gold medal tonight as he swam the butterfly leg of the winning United States 400-meter medley relay team. And for the seventh time in these Olympic Games, the 22-year-old Spitz was in on a world record.

A native of California who attended Indiana University, Spitz also set world marks in the individual 100- and 200-meter freestyle events, the 100- and 200-meter butterfly races, and in anchoring the winning 400-meter and 800-meter freestyle relay teams.

The 6-foot, 160-pound Spitz—whose extraordinarily long legs enable him to kick deeper in the water than most swimmers—is the first individual to win seven gold medals in a single Olympic Games. Three others had won as many as five, but no one had ever won more than that.

Most gold medals, one Olympics: 7, Mark Spitz, United States, 1972

CYCLING

An American First in Paris

PARIS, France, July 27, 1986—An American today won the Tour de France—the world's most prestigious bicycle race—for the first time since the event was inaugurated in 1903.

Greg LeMond, a 25-year-old native of Nevada who now calls Sacramento, Cal., and Kortrijk, Belgium, home, pedaled down the Champs Elysées before 200,000 cheering spectators as the overall winner of the grueling race, which began July 4. The race is conducted in individual sections, or legs, on a 2,500-mile course that roughly circumnavigates France, starting and ending in Paris and including arduous stretches in the Pyrenees Mountains near the Spanish border and the Alps near the Swiss border.

LeMond finished the race with a total elapsed time of 110 hours, 35 minutes, and 19 seconds, which was 3 minutes, 10 seconds ahead of his mentor and teammate Bernard Hinault of the Vie Claire team. Hinault has won the Tour de France a record-tying five times.

A former U.S. Olympic team cyclist, Gregory James LeMond grew up in northwestern Nevada, where he had originally wanted to be a downhill skier and took up cycling as an offseason training activity.

First American to win the Tour de France: Gregory LeMond, July 27, 1986

Greg LeMond (left) edged France's Bernard Hinault to become the first American to win the Tour de France.   *Wide World*

SPEED SKATING

Heiden's Sweep on Ice

LAKE PLACID, N.Y., Feb. 23, 1980—He'd already won four gold medals in Olympic-record time at 500 meters, 1,000, 1,500, and 5,000. And now Eric Heiden was at the starting line for the 10,000-meter speed-skating race, the most grueling of all, in the Winter Olympic Games.

The 21-year-old from Madison, Wis., proceeded to go faster today than anyone on speed skates ever has for 10,000 meters. He broke the world record by six seconds (14:28.13) as he skated to an unprecedented fifth gold medal, the most anyone has ever achieved in a Winter Olympics.

Most gold medals, one Winter Olympics: 5, Eric Heiden, 500 meters,
1,000, 1,500, 5,000, 10,000, Feb. 15–23, 1980

Eric Heiden won five Olympic gold medals at Lake Placid in 1980. *UPI*

About the Authors

Zander Hollander is president of Associated Features, specialists in sports publishing. He is coauthor of *The Sports Nostalgia Quiz Book* series, edits *The Complete Handbook of Baseball, Pro Football, Pro Basketball* and *Hockey,* and has edited six sports encyclopedias. He was a sportswriter on the late *New York World-Telegram and Sun.*

David Schulz, coauthor of *The Sports Nostalgia Quiz Book* series, has written several books on sports, travel, and other leisure-oriented activities. He has been a contributing editor to *Fodor's Travel Guides,* the *Birnbaum Travel Guides* and the 20-volume series, *The Ocean World of Jacques Cousteau,* several sports encyclopedias, and short story collections. He wrote sports for the Associated Press and was a staffer on *The Morning Telegraph.*

Totally revised and updated for sports fans,
nostalgia buffs, and trivia game players ...

THE SPORTS NOSTALGIA
QUIZ BOOK
Revised and Updated
Zander Hollander and
David Schulz

What does Gorgeous George have in common
with Joe DiMaggio? Wilt Chamberlain with
Ring Lardner? Jack Dempsey with Tarzan? Bill
Tilden with the Galloping Ghost? Answer:
They're all among the cast of thousands in THE
SPORTS NOSTALGIA QUIZ BOOK, the perfect
game book to be played off the field, in the
clubhouse or recreation room, and between
innings, beers and brawls! Over 1,900 teasers
for recall and replay—famed athletes,
outstanding competitions, and unusual outcomes
are given as questions, answers, or clues.

There's an epidemic with 27 million victims. And no visible symptoms.

It's an epidemic of people who can't read.

Believe it or not, 27 million Americans are functionally illiterate, about one adult in five.

The solution to this problem is you... when you join the fight against illiteracy. So call the Coalition for Literacy at toll-free **1-800-228-8813** and volunteer.

Volunteer Against Illiteracy. The only degree you need is a degree of caring.